THE TEAM OF '66

THE TEAM OF '66

England's World Cup Winners and the Story of Their Success

JIM MORRIS

AMBERLEY

First published 2014

Amberley Publishing
The Hill, Stroud
Gloucestershire, GL5 4EP

www.amberley-books.com

British Library Cataloguing in Publication Data.
A catalogue record for this book is available from the British Library.

ISBN 978 1 4456 3666 5

Typeset in 10pt on 12pt Sabon.
Typesetting and Origination by Amberley Publishing.
Printed in the UK.

CONTENTS

Note on the Text

The natural way to set this book out seemed to be by the numbering on the shirts the players wore, but it starts with the man who would select the players to occupy the shirts, and then the men who coached and trained them. They are followed by the twenty-two players in order of their shirt number. Each is a separate story, so various approaches are employed: with some I can slot their England games into their otherwise chronological life. With others a less rigid chronological approach might deal with a catalogue of club success and then their international success. Managerial or other roles in the game came later in their lives, and one of the players had a fabulous club and international career as a player and the same in his role as manager.

There are a few more people worthy of a quick word. Alf Ramsey and his coaching staff were loosely described as the back room boys, but then there were others who linked the squad and the players with the millions of people watching the unfolding tournament on the telly, and as tellys were often in peoples' front room then they might be called the 'front room boys': the likes of Kenneth Wolstenholme and Hugh Johns are part of our memories of the tournament.

There was also, for the first time, a World Cup mascot who has an interesting pedigree: World Cup Willie was a lion in a football shirt. Although mascots didn't appear until 1966 they have been in every tournament since.

Introduction

As each decade passes a group of words may become popular and a few drop off the side of the world, but one word which wasn't bandied about with the same freedom fifty years ago as it is today is 'icon'. England wasn't short of them in the 1960s – we had The Beatles, Cliff, The Stones; we had Richard Burton and Elizabeth Taylor and the Laurences: Harvey and Olivier. They were 'stars'; they were 'fab'. But were they 'icons'? And would such a term ever be associated with men who, in cold, wet and muddy conditions competed for a goal or two on a Saturday afternoon? The answer to this is yes, even if it wasn't applied at the time – because in 1966 twenty-two men in shirts, three in tracksuits, two with microphones and a cartoon character, elevated English football onto its highest plain, a place where, sadly, it hasn't been since.

They won the World Cup. It wasn't just the goal scorers and the goal savers though – or the eleven led by Bobby Moore who defeated the world's best. It was the whole squad and the back room boys who achieved it. The television had entered a lot of houses by the mid-sixties and televised football was gaining ground – and the England squad actually included the first man to score a goal in a televised league match.

Off-field publicity wasn't new as football cards had been in cigarette packets for years, but they now began to find their way into bubble-gum packets and so into the kids' world. Comics appeared more commonly too, where footballing heroes could score a last minute winner, or pass a ball forty yards with breath-taking accuracy, or save a goal with incredible agility. The reason for this was that there were real players actually doing this almost routinely, and when they got together under the right management, then winning the World Cup might have been inevitable. Plain Mr Alf Ramsey had said so when appointed to the England Manager's job. He had a philosophy that the more players got to know each other and the more they understood each other's game then the more likely it was that they would form a world-beating spirit – the only time they might have doubted this was immediately after the ninety minutes of the 1966 World Cup final, before extra time. Alf's words were simple: 'You've won it once, now go out and win it again'. And they did. Suddenly the pop stars and the acting greats were joined by their peers in football. And footballers were to become the new stars.

This book is about twenty-two Sixties footballers. With their strength, courage, grit, determination and skill: it is, therefore, a tribute to all of them.

THE BACKROOM BOYS: MANAGEMENT, TRAINING AND COACHING

Alf Ramsey – Team Manager

Winning the League Championship is nearly every football manager's dream, though few have won it more than once, or with two different clubs. Even fewer have won it with a team built up locally and without a large row of noughts on a cheque. But what Ipswich Town had in Alf Ramsey was a leader with infinite man management skills and one who could spot footballing talent a mile off in heavy fog, who then knew how to build a team and press all the right buttons to make it win.

Yet the paradox of Alf Ramsey is the feeling, even among those who one would think knew him best, that they didn't truly know him. For someone who wanted to foster a family set-up where the players regarded each other as friends as well as team-mates, few people have said they knew him as a friend. This might suggest he was viewed with some level of awe. Even after his death, as the fiftieth anniversary of England's win approaches, few of the players he worked with at club or international level have had a single bad word for him.

As far as Alf was concerned, it was the players who were important. This didn't make him too many friends at the Football Association (FA): it must have grated with some to see the triumph that the country and the national sport craved so much come from Alf.

Alfred Ernest Ramsey was born in Dagenham, Essex on 22 January, 1920 and died in Ipswich, Suffolk on 28 April, 1999. Alf started life in the grocery business, though he was a keen amateur footballer.

He played for Portsmouth in the London War League in 1942 before moving to Southampton from 1943 to 1949, turning professional in 1944, playing at right back. He went to Tottenham Hotspur where he made over 250 appearances in the league and FA Cup, and in 1951 they won the League Championship.

In 1948 Alf made his England debut against Switzerland; he captained his country three times. His last international was the six-three defeat by Hungary in November 1953 in which he scored a penalty. In total he was capped thirty-two times and scored three goals, each from the penalty spot. Alf had excellent positional sense, read the game better than most, had awareness, strength and excellent distribution.

He played his last match in 1955 and become manager of Ipswich Town. He guided them to third place in the

Third Division south, they scored 106 goals in forty-six league fixtures. In Alf's second season at Portman Road, 1956/57, the club won the Third Division championship, and promotion to the Second Division.

After three seasons in the Second Division where Ipswich Town established themselves as mid-table occupants, Alf and his players cranked up their performance and won the Second Division title. At the end of the season 1960/61 they were promoted to the First Division. The club were tipped to be relegated the following year but, much to the delight of Suffolk, they won the League Championship. Winning the League Championship is an accolade in itself, but this was a remarkable achievement.

Alf's tactical astuteness, working with a squad of solid but not outstanding players, astonished the illustrious football clubs whom Ipswich were playing. He had found the style he would later bring to the England Manager's job; choosing players to fit his system on the pitch. He left Ipswich Town on 29 April, 1963.

At the heart of his success was a new style of play he'd pioneered without wingers, as Alf felt they couldn't drop back to support the defence as readily as a midfield player. So he nurtured attacking midfielders who could also drop back, should the need arise. This system allowed attacking midfielders and strikers to take the ball through the middle. This style of play proved successful at Ipswich, but on the international stage it was a revolution. In Spain, after a friendly, Bobby Charlton remarked, 'The Spanish full backs were just looking at each other while we were going in droves through the middle'.

Alf's appointment as England Manager was made on 25 October, 1962 but due to club commitments he didn't take up the post until 1 May, 1963. He predicted England would win the next World Cup, which was to be held in England in 1966. He achieved control over squad selections, which hitherto had been made by a panel and he was a firm but fair manager: he made sure that no-one felt that they enjoyed special status, star player or not. His strict regime didn't suit everyone but the players with respect for the game responded and had great respect for him. His decision to appoint a young Bobby Moore as captain also showed ability to see potential in young players.

The 1966 World Cup opened with a drab display against Uruguay but Alf still used a winger for each group game: John Connelly, Terry Paine and Ian Callaghan. He also juggled Alan Ball and Martin Peters in midfield. Wins against Mexico and France ensured progression, but not without incident – FIFA didn't like Nobby Stiles' play. There had been a late tackle against Jacques Simon in the French tie. But Alf did like Nobby's play: so that dealt with that. He also kept Geoff Hurst in the team when Jimmy Greaves even after regained his fitness: Alf wouldn't change a winning team.

He did change tactics, though, putting Nobby Stiles, Bobby Charlton, Martin Peters and Alan Ball in midfield. It was enough to beat the Argentinians in the quarter-finals, though they'd effectively thrown the match away.

England were solid in defence with no goals conceded, in control in midfield and with goal-scoring forwards.

The side was settled. The 'real final' they say was against Portugal in the semis, which was a superb display.

The final was won in extra time because Alf knew there was still power in his players' legs. Physical fitness and tactics, he'd always said: 'Soccer is a simple game.'

In the European Championships in 1968 England finished third: 'Third place in Europe is not our place.'

In 1970 England qualified for the World Cup finals in Mexico as holders. They won two of the three group games by a single goal and lost the third by a single goal. Their play was creative but, when beaten by West Germany in the quarter-finals, one might have thought the rot had set in. In truth the trouble had started long before: Alf was a footballer not a politician and didn't much care for the hierarchy at the FA. And they wanted him out.

The 1972 European Championships were won by West Germany who beat England convincingly at Wembley but were held to a nil-nil draw in Berlin.

In the 1974 World Cup qualifiers England drew Wales and Poland. Poland won their leg in Katowice but England failed to beat them at Wembley, so it was Poland who qualified. They were skilful and their goalkeeper Jan Tomelaszewski could probably have saved two shots at once, such was his game. England had some bad luck and did everything but win.

Alf was therefore sacked. It was openly said that some FA officials had long held grudges against him, particularly the FA chief Harold Thompson.

After Alf left the job England were left in the doldrums, much as Ipswich Town were after he left. When he was offered the England Manager's job he had a talk with the Ipswich Town chairman John Cobbold, who advised Alf to take it although he must have known a replacement would be impossible to secure. They did get the former England star Jackie Milburn but after a couple of seasons the side were back in the Second Division. Following a particularly bad game at Fulham John Cobbold said, 'The game could have gone either way – before it started.' Fulham won by ... ten goals to one: George Cohen was there that day.

Alf Ramsey managed England for 113 games: he had won sixty-nine, drew twenty-seven and lost seventeen, yet he was not consulted again in any capacity by the FA after his sacking. He never fully recovered from this shabby treatment. Alf retired from football to Ipswich, where he concentrated on golf. He came out of retirement briefly to manage Birmingham City in 1977 before resigning because of ill-health.

He married Victoria Answorth in 1951 and they had a daughter. Alf was knighted in 1967 in recognition of England's World Cup win.

Sir Bobby Robson, who also managed both Ipswich Town and England, said that Alf was the greatest manager English football ever had.

It's curious that if people are asked about Don Revie they talk about Leeds United, if asked about Ron Greenwood they mention West Ham. But mention Alf Ramsey and they talk about the World Cup.

Harold Shepherdson
– Trainer/Coach

Ayresome Street is still there, as is Clive Road. And between the two was Ayresome Park. Some of the greatest to grace the Ayresome Park pitch are commemorated there: Brian Clough, George Camsell and Willie Maddren all have their names on street signs – but Harold Shepherdson was the unsung hero of Middlesbrough, a club he served as supporter, player, trainer and caretaker-manager. Today, Shepherdson Way is the road to take you to the current headquarters of Middlesbrough FC at the Riverside Stadium.

His parents, Joseph and Jane started their married life in Pearl Street but, by the time Harold was born in October 1918, they had moved to Elm Street. As a schoolboy he loved cricket and football but his professional playing days were to be interrupted by the Second World War, in which he served with the Royal Green Jackets as a physical training instructor. When peace came there was only one place he wanted to go and that was home to Middlesbrough, but a knee injury put paid to his playing career and he was to find his true strengths in training; he was said to be an expert in fitness and training techniques.

Harold married Margaret (Peggy) Martin in 1940 and they had three daughters, Valerie, Linda and Margaret, all of whom grew up in Middlesbrough, married there and settled.

In total Harold made 171 'appearances' as England trainer – from 1958 when England defeated Scotland by four goals to nil at Hampden Park, right through to their draw with Poland in 1974. He worked under Walter Winterbottom and Alf Ramsey. He was ever present on the bench during the 1966 finals. Alf later said that without Harold's input England wouldn't have won.

He was awarded the MBE in 1969 for his services to football.

Harold left the international scene in the mid-Seventies, at about the same time as Alf was relieved of his duties as England manager, but he continued his work at Middlesbrough, becoming caretaker manager three times – in fact he resisted a few temptations to manage other clubs. His final retirement came in 1983, back where he had started out – Middlesbrough's Ayrsome Park.

Harold passed away aged 76 in September 1995 and Peggy followed him in 2011, but along the way she picked up a World Cup winners medal on his behalf in 2009 in a special ceremony in Dowling Street. Peggy was also a committed Middlesbrough supporter and attended games well into her eighties. Their middle daughter Linda is married to a former Middlesbrough full back.

Les Cocker – Trainer/ Coach

Frank and Ellen Cocker had settled in Stockport in Cheshire and were employed in the millenary industry. They had two daughters and a son, Leslie. He was born in 1924 so was too young to enlist at the outbreak of war, but he did serve later and, when he came home to Stockport, he was taken on by Stockport County as a professional footballer in 1946.

Les married Nora Pickersgill in 1950 and three sons came along in the next eight years or so.

His playing career started with Stockport County, for which he scored a total of forty-three goals over seven seasons. County were typically mid-table while Les was with them, but they did have two good seasons, finishing in the top four in the old Third Division (North).

In 1953 he moved to Accrington Stanley where he had a slightly better strike rate with forty-eight goals in 122 appearances. Stanley were usually near the top of the Third Division (North) but didn't ever progress.

Les hung up his boots in 1958 and travelled south to become trainer at Luton Town in August 1959, mainly under Syd Owen. In the early 1960s, though, he went back north to the Rugby League stronghold of Leeds. Leeds United were a Second Division club with a centre forward called Don Revie who became player-manager before taking the full managerial job. They formed a partnership that took Leeds to just about every domestic success possible, and Les was also appointed as an England trainer under Walter Winterbottom. He stayed with the England International set-up and when Alf Ramsey took the team to victory in the 1966 finals, he was right there with him.

Les had a collection of travelling tea-pots, and he always brought one along so he could always have a decent brew, wherever he was for an international. It was called the world's most travelled tea-pot. Les also lent his tea and sympathy to John Spencer, the England rugby captain, when he sustained a hamstring injury. Spencer recalled, 'Now I know what they mean by professional treatment. Les Cocker has been absolutely magnificent in getting my hamstring right.' So there was far more to the trainer's roll than just the magic sponge.

Les used to attend matches assessing potential Leeds and England stars. One such was Albert Johannson who, with Les, Don and the lads, and fans at Leeds United, paved the way for ethnic diversity in football. His signing was one small step for Leeds, one giant leap for world football.

When Don Revie took the England manager's job in 1974, Les was appointed as assistant manager and went on to train the United Arab Emirates side in 1977 with Don. He returned to Yorkshire in 1979 to Doncaster Rovers who had appointed former Leeds United magician Billy Bremner as manager. Sadly in October of 1979 Les passed away.

He wasn't forgotten, though, either by Leeds United or the country: following a sustained campaign the back room boys and non-final players of 1966 were belatedly, in Les's case posthumously, awarded a World Cup winner's medal in 2009.

THE STARS;
THE ICONS

1

Gordon Banks – Goalkeeper

There is unlikely to be anyone living or dead who would dispute that England had the best goalkeeper in the world at the time in Gordon Banks. He let in fewer goals than his peers, the closest rival being the Russian Lev Yashin. He was beaten only three times in the tournament: once by a Eusabio penalty, by a goal set up by an England defender, and by the West German equaliser in the final after a dubious free-kick and a goal-mouth scramble. He didn't make his greatest ever save in this tournament – that was perhaps from Denis Law the following year, or against Pele four years later – but Gordon's contribution to the win was without doubt.

One would need an entire book to list Gordon Banks's attributes but he was England's best, which is the main reason Peter Bonetti secured fewer caps than his skills would have suggested, and why Ron Springett's reign as England No. 1 was so brief.

Gordon was a Sheffield lad, born in late December 1937, the youngest of four brothers. He learnt his skills on Tinsley 'rec' and was selected, then de-selected, for Sheffield Boys. But you can't keep a good lad down and after leaving school he worked briefly for a coal merchants before becoming a brick laying apprentice. He was spotted by Chesterfield, for whom he made his debut in November 1958; this coming after his National Service. Gordon soon became their regular selection. But Leicester City, a strong First Division club, came hunting and he soon established himself there despite an abundance of goalkeepers on the club's books. A couple of Wembley finals and a close call with the league and FA Cup double showed the other clubs that Leicester City was a team to beat. Leicester beat his later club Stoke City over two legs in the Football League Cup final but were defeated by Chelsea the following year.

Gordon's career saw him make a total of seventy-three appearances for England and he was ever-present during the World Cup finals in 1966, keeping a clean sheet throughout the group stage and in the quarter-final against Argentina. Then Jack Charlton made a great diving save to fist the ball off the line against Portugal in the semi-final, leaving Gordon to face a penalty. But as he said, the result of every penalty should be a goal, and so it was when Eusabio buried the ball to the opposite side Alan Ball had suggested. Gordon's clean sheet was gone.

Then just before full time, with England hanging on for a win against the Portuguese, Jack Charlton was beaten in the air but Nobby Stiles got back to cover. Mario Coluna nearly caught Gordon off his guard, but they held on.

Gordon Banks became the first English goalkeeper to win a World Cup winner's medal, a record that stood until 2009 when it was decreed by FIFA that all players in the squad should receive a medal, so that Peter Bonetti and Ron Springett also received their accolade.

He finished his playing career at Stoke City and Gordon lives with his wife Ursula in Cheshire, with their three grown up children nearby.

2

George Cohen – Defender: Right Back

George Cohen was born on 22 October 1939 in Kensington, London, and grew up in the capital. When he was ready to turn professional in 1956 he made his career plans around Fulham, where he would spend his whole playing career. George Best, who had the most incredible ball control, balance and agility and who could run rings around most defenders, said that George 'was the best full back I ever played against.' Alf described him as 'England's greatest right back.' At club level George didn't win any trophies, but that was through bad luck: Fulham had some great stars in their line-up in the early Sixties such as Rodney Marsh, Alan Mullery, Alan Clarke, Bobby Robson and England's first £100 a week star Johnny Haynes, who George said was the best player he played alongside during his club days.

At international level he was restricted to a handful of caps at under-23 level but by May 1964, with regular right back Jimmy Armfield injured, George made his full debut in a two goals to one win over Uruguay; a friendly at Wembley. Following this, England defeated Portugal on their own territory in Lisbon where, even with three goals conceded, the England defence was considered as 'resilient'. George went on to play in twenty-one of the next twenty-three internationals. In a 'mini-World Cup' tournament in Brazil in 1964 he gave way to Bobby Thomson of Wolverhampton Wanderers (record holder of caps at under-23 level) for two games, but Alf had wanted the whole squad to get a game. In England's final match at Wembley before the World Cup finals, Jimmy Armfield came into the side for a two-nil win against Yugoslavia, and in the short Scandinavian tour that followed, Jimmy was again in the No. 2 shirt for a three-nil win against Finland. But George was back for the final three games of the short tour, which saw England score twelve goals to one against. He was, therefore, Alf Ramsey's first choice for right back when the 1966 World Cup finals started. It wasn't easy for any of the players in the squad: 'We'd all had a long season, playing something like fifty-five games. It had been a hard slog before we started preparing for the World Cup.' But there was a belief among the squad, a belief in themselves: 'We were very confident. Sir Alf instilled that into us.'

His speedy performances enhanced the others and made sure George was present throughout the group games and for the knockout stage. He blended well with Alf's desire to play four at the back, four in the middle and two up front. Along with Ray Wilson, his opposite number at left back, he could take the ball forward as a 'winger' as well as look after things at the back. It's possible Jack Charlton and Bobby Moore on their own were worth four at the back – but if the opposition got through them they still had Gordon to contend with! George seemed to take the Argentinian quarter-final tie as just another game and seemed surprised Alf didn't want him to swap shirts at the end – sadly this incident has become one of the more notorious of the tournament, captured vividly in a photograph. If Argentina had played to their strength, which was football, and not to their weaknesses, gamesmanship, England would have been severely tested.

The final for which he was vice-captain was his thirtieth cap. When the teams left their dressing rooms for the final George was struck by the fact that he couldn't hear anything, but as they headed for the pitch, 'I heard this buzzing like a bee. The buzzing became a roar. When I got to the pitch all I could see was movement and colour. That was the only time I felt nervous.' He described the pitch on the day of the final as 'spongy': there had been a mixture of weather. The pitch tended to hold the boots of the players and slow them fractionally but the ball tended to skim on the wet surface. More than one player and former player have said this gave England the advantage. 'Sir Alf said to us that the West Germans were finished.' Helmut Schoen, the West German manager, was gracious in defeat and said England deserved to win.

George won seven more caps for England, the last of which was in November 1967 against Northern Ireland at Wembley: Keith Newton and Cyril Knowles (both of whom are no longer with us) were beginning to knock on the door.

George remained first choice full back for Fulham until March 1969, but he retired from playing due to injury. He had made 459 appearances for Fulham, and scored six goals.

He remained in football for a short while and coached the Fulham youth team and the England under-23 team. He also managed non-league side Tonbridge.

George wasn't one to court the limelight, but being a full back and a 'winger' his playing speaks for itself. His World Cup winner's medal now belongs to Fulham Football Club, where there is a George Cohen Restaurant. When the non-playing members of the team were presented with medals in 2009 George attended the ceremony and collected Alf Ramsey's medal on behalf of his family.

He does think it might be difficult for an England side to win the World Cup again, which he has said is due to the amount of players in the top flight who wouldn't be able to play for England due to their nationality. George has said that with an influx of players from other countries it tends to hinder the opportunities for younger players to get premier league experience.

It is less of a physical game now than it was, which has been helped by better facilities: pitches are far less liable to be turned into a bog by the second game of the season and changes to the ball have helped too. But he would remind us that some great players emerged in those days, and that we may not have seen their like since. One would have to say he has got a point.

He received the MBE in the Millennium honours, which was long overdue. Four others from the team joined him that day, following a media campaign for the 'forgotten five'.

George married Daphne Church in September 1962 and they had two sons, Anthony and Andrew. Now they have a collection of grandchildren too. Sports icons seem to run in George's family, as his nephew Ben Cohen is an England Rugby international.

George had a long battle with bowel cancer from which he has now had the all-clear. Bobby Moore was not so lucky with the same disease.

3

Ray Wilson – Defender: Left Back

Ramon Wilson was born in Shirebrook in Derbyshire on 17 December 1934, and was Alf's preferred left back. He'd played at inside left and at left half before going to the No 3, but it was there that he shined as a true craftsman.

He started work on the railways when he first left school but was football mad and when spotted by a scout for Huddersfield Town the rest, as they say, is history. He worked nights to support himself and then trained in the daytime, a routine that was interrupted only by National Service. Ray would later say that training under Alf at Lilleshall was like doing National Service. However he returned to Huddersfield – he had been in Egypt with the Royal Artillery – and made his debut for Huddersfield Town in a defeat at the hands of Manchester United in 1955. That didn't bother Ray or the then manager Bill Shankly. He was soon to become the first choice Huddersfield Town left back, and stayed there for twelve years – Harry Catterick was unsuccessful when he wanted to take him to Sheffield Wednesday, but did succeed later with Everton.

Ray made 266 appearances for Huddersfield Town, and scored six goals. He was capped on thirty occasions for England while at Leeds Road and remains the clubs highest capped player for England.

He joined Everton in a £40,000 package late in 1964, which was a record for a full back at the time. He was in good company for his debut just under a week before Christmas – at the back with him was Tommy Wright and Brian Labone. 41,994 folk saw Jimmy Greaves score twice for Tottenham Hotspur, and Fred Pickering score twice for Everton. Disappointment followed because Ray missed the final six games of the 1964/65 season, but he was back the following August.

And he was a rock against Sheffield Wednesday at Wembley in the FA Cup final of May 1966, making his first lap of honour at the hallowed ground in the blue shirt of Everton. Jim McCalliog had put Sheffield Wednesday into the lead, which was consolidated by David Ford in the second half: Everton's Alex Young had put the ball in the net but was offside. But as soon as Everton had their backs against the wall they really started to play. Mike Trebilcock beat Ron Springett with a fine drive and then blasted one in from the edge of the eighteen-yard box. So two goals each: Everton were 'twice the team they'd been in the first half.' Derek Temple hammered home the winner to give Ray his first cup winner's medal of that summer. Just eleven weeks later he made another lap of honour at Wembley, showing the Jules Rimet Trophy to the World.

He would later point out that Everton won the league title a year before he went there and again a year after he'd left, but he was to make 116 appearances for Everton, though he didn't score any goals. He was unlucky with injuries as his career matured and he was given a free transfer to Oldham Athletic in 1969. He retired through injury in 1971 following twenty-five games for Oldham and then two for Bradford City – for whom he acted as caretaker manager for a couple of months before he finally called it a day.

His international career had started in April 1960 in a one-one draw with Scotland. He was to be a regular under Walter Winterbottom and Alf Ramsey –favoured by the selection panel in Walter's tenure and left back for England through the group games and the quarter-final in Chile in 1962.

In 1966 Ray was the ultimate choice at full back. Against Portugal in the semi-finals Ray made his fiftieth appearance for England. And he is owed a favour by the West German side as it was Ray who headed the ball down for Helmut Haller to score the opening goal in the final. He said later that he was the senior or oldest player, so his experience would let him put it behind him and get on with the match. He was about a hairs-breadth from clearing in the goal-mouth scramble in the last seconds when Wolfgang Weber equalised for West Germany.

Ray continued in his No. 3 shirt right through to the third place play-off in the European Championships in 1968, his sixty-third and final England cap. He didn't score any goals for his country.

He never liked the limelight and preferred the quiet life. After his footballing career he built up a successful undertakers business in Halifax, from which he finally retired in 1997.

In 2000 he joined the other forgotten few from 1966 when he was awarded an MBE for his services to football.

Ramon married Patricia Lumb in Huddersfield in 1956 and had two sons: Russell and Neil.

He is remembered as one of the best left backs that England ever produced, possessing vision, pin-point passing ability and strong runs as an acting left winger. It made him an important member of the 1966 World Cup squad, and he is considered as one of the greatest ever players to don a Huddersfield Town or Everton shirt.

He said of that day in 1966: 'I think it moves me more now than it did then. It has got more important. I do find it much more difficult to sit and watch it on the television and see me standing there, and the Queen, and I'm thinking – and I do, I say it to myself – how the hell did you do that?'

4
Nobby Stiles – Midfielder: Defence Support

Norbert Peter Stiles was born in Collyhurst in Manchester on 18 May 1942, the day incidentally that competitive baseball was put on hold in the United States until the end of the war.

Nobby played for England for five years, and won twenty-eight caps. He scored a single goal in what became known as the World Cup rehearsal against West Germany at Wembley on 23 February 1966. Nobby was in his No. 4 shirt for every minute in the 1966 finals and is probably best remembered by the public on the day of the final as he danced around the pitch on the team's lap of honour holding the Cup aloft. Other people might remember his toothless smile but Alf Ramsey smiled in the semi-finals because he simply didn't let Eusabio have half an inch of space. In fact the only time he let the Portuguese master have a clear shot at goal was when they were awarded a penalty for Jack Charlton's acrobatic dive to save a certain goal. In the final he'd double charged his batteries: he just didn't stop running. Nobby would always work to get the ball back from the opposition.

He was born, bred and buttered in Manchester, grew up in Collyhurst and supported Manchester United as a lad. His brother Charles was four years older. Nobby played for England Schoolboys at the age of 15 and was taken on at Old Trafford as an apprentice in September 1959. He spent eleven years at Old Trafford, where he became renowned for his tough tackling and ball-winning qualities.

Short in stature and quite a wiry character, he became a giant on the pitch where he saw everything, even though he suffered from severe short-sightedness: he needed contact lenses to play and wore a trademark large pair of spectacles off the field. Manchester United manager Matt Busby saw something in the tenacious youngster and he made his debut in October 1960, in front of 39,197 at Burnden Park in Bolton. His future brother-in-law Johnny Giles scored for Manchester United – Nobby married Kay the following year and they were to have three sons, one of whom played for Leeds United after his uncle Johnny Giles had left!

Although he wore the No. 4 shirt, which was regarded as a half-back in those days, people like Alf Ramsey were changing the formations of the sides. Alf was famous for having two up front with a midfield of four, and

Nobby was one of the early exponents of a 'holding' midfielder. He could gain and retain possession, which gave his front men the chance to create some space for themselves and each other. But he was also a good defender, and his one-on-one marking was above world class.

From his absence in the 1963 FA Cup final until the championship-winning season of 1964/65, Nobby was to become a permanent fixture in Manchester United's games. Not surprisingly he started to wear the senior shirts with three lions on them.

England didn't need to go through the qualifying rounds in the World Cup so Alf could experiment with his team and fine tune them – Bobby Charlton was effectively an attacking midfielder, but it's curious that Alf was still using a couple of players who were out-and-out wing players, though Ian Callaghan was to have almost a second career in a midfield role.

Through the early months of 1966 England had eight friendlies and Home Internationals so Nobby was well exposed to the team building – he even scored a goal (as did Bobby Moore). It was no surprise to find him in Alf Ramsey's final selection of the twenty-two squad members.

As for the first match against Uruguay, they fielded ten defenders and a goalkeeper, Nobby enjoyed a leisurely work-out for his fifteenth cap and Alf was pleased with the performance, if not the result. In the second match against Mexico the dye was cast and few got through the midfield, let alone the back four.

He's been called a 'hard man' but this is badly aimed criticism: he was a robust tackler so if he was a half a second late it could be misconstrued. Probably the most notorious example was in the World Cup group match against France. About twenty minutes from time Jacques Simon took possession. Nobby was just late with his tackle – and it upset Nobby as much as anyone; but Alf, who came under pressure to drop Nobby from the team, was having none of it. He was, according to Alf, a world class player and even if not the type to be a household name like other Manchester United icons of the time, he could pass and work for other players. He could play a ball first time from nothing into a goal scoring chance and he made it look so easy.

If success can be measured in medals then Nobby had a World Cup winner's medal, a European Cup winner's medal and a couple of League Championships: that can argue against any criticism.

And so about two years after holding up that twelve-inch trophy, Nobby could hold aloft the European Cup. Poor old Eusabio (RIP) must have wondered if he was in for as lean a time for Benfica against Manchester United as he'd had for Portugal against England – he was, and in extra time three goals were enough to take the European Cup to England for the first time.

But not the European Championship, and England finished in third place. Nobby was beginning to move aside for Alan Mullery, though he was in the squad for the Mexico finals in 1970. Nobby made his final appearance for England in a goalless draw at Hampden Park in April

1970 which was his twenty-eighth cap; of all in the World Cup final in 1966, he was the least capped.

Nobby left Manchester United in 1971. He had made 392 appearances and scored nineteen goals, but Matt Busby had too many talented youngsters and said when the fee of £25,000 was agreed that Middlesbrough were getting him for nothing! He made fifty-seven appearances for Middlesbrough. Two years later he was back in Lancashire with Preston North End – for whom he made forty-six appearances, with Bobby Charlton as manager, but the two left the club after some disagreements with directors. Nobby became a manager but it didn't suit him – he was very meek on the touchline. He returned to Preston as manager for four years from 1977, then he took his skills and experience to Canada.

Management wasn't good for his health and West Bromwich Albion may have done him a big favour when they let him go in 1986 after only a few months – but he never seemed to settle out of Lancashire, and specifically Manchester. He was to return to Old Trafford to coach the likes of Paul Scholes, David Beckham, Ryan Giggs and others.

He picked up his MBE in 2000.

Nobby was paid £3 5s 0d (£3.25) a week when he started at Manchester United, and when he signed for Middlesbrough in 1971 he was paid about £20,000 a year. He later sold his memorabilia for far more than he earned in his entire playing career.

At the time of writing Nobby had just been diagnosed with prostate cancer, which is treatable and men can recover, so we can all hope for the best – he owes the world nothing, in fact it's us that owe him. One story from 1966 has no doubt been added to and edited over the past forty-odd years: As the wives were almost beside themselves with pleasure and probably a bit of relief at the end of extra time, Nobby's wife just had one wish – and it was that Nobby would put his false teeth back in!

5

Jack Charlton – Defender: Centre Half

John Charlton was born on 8 May 1935 and spent his entire club career – from 1950 to 1973 – with Leeds United. They won the Second Division title 1963/64, the First Division title 1968/69, FA Cup 1972, Football League Cup 1968, Charity Shield 1969, Inter-City Fairs Cup 1968 and 1971, as well as another promotion from the Second Division 1955/56. His 762 appearances are a club record, and Leeds supporters voted Jack into the club's greatest ever XI in 2006.

He was called up to the England team just before his 30th birthday, and went on to score six goals in 35 international games, and to appear in two World Cups and one European Championship. He was named by the Football Writers' Association as Footballer of the Year in 1967.

After retiring as a player he worked as a manager, and led Middlesbrough to the Second Division title in 1973/74, winning the Manager of the Year award in his first season. Jack kept Middlesbrough as a stable top-flight club before he resigned in April 1977. He took charge of Sheffield Wednesday in October 1977 and led the club to promotion out of the Third Division in 1979/80. He left Hillsborough in May 1983 and went on to serve Middlesbrough as caretaker-manager at the end of the 1983/84 season. He was Newcastle United manager for the 1984/85 season. He took charge of the Republic of Ireland national team in February 1986 and led them to their first ever World Cup finals in 1990, where they reached the quarter-finals. He also led the nation to successful qualification to Euro 1988 and to the 1994 World Cup. He finally retired in January 1996.

Jack grew up in Ashington, Northumberland and was initially overshadowed by his younger brother Bobby, who was taken on by Manchester United while Jack did National Service with the Household Cavalry. The Milburn lads were part of their mother's extended family.

Ashington was a coal-mining town and his father was a miner with no interest in football, but their mother, Cissie, played football with her children and later coached the local schools team. As teenagers she took them to watch Ashington and Newcastle United play; Jack has remained a lifelong Newcastle supporter.

He was offered a trial at Leeds United, but turned it down and instead joined his father down the mine. That didn't last long. He applied to join the police and reconsidered the offer from Leeds. His trial game for Leeds clashed with his police interview, so he chose football and so became part of Elland Road folklore.

Jack soon graduated to the third team in the Yorkshire League, and at just sixteen impressed the club's management, so was soon promoted to the reserve team. Manager Raich Carter handed him his first professional contract at seventeen.

He made his debut on 25 April 1953 against Doncaster Rovers, taking John Charles's place at centre-half: John moved up to centre forward. It was the final Second Division game of the 1952/53 season, and ended in a goalless draw. In National Service he captained his regiment to victory in the Cavalry Cup. His National Service limited his contribution to Leeds, and he made only one appearance in the 1954/55 season.

But he was a regular in the first team in the 1955/56 season, helping win promotion into the First Division. He was dropped in the second half of the 1956/57 campaign: he was a sociable lad and lost focus on his football. He regained his place in the next season, and settled down to married life: he'd married Pat in 1958.

Leeds struggled after Raich Carter left in 1958, as neither team manager Willis Edwards or then Bill Lambton set the world alight, and in the 1958/59 season Leeds hovered above the relegation zone. Jack Taylor was appointed manager, but failed to keep Leeds away from relegation at the end of the 1959/60 season. Jack was taking his career seriously, with coaching in mind, and he took the FA's coaching courses at Lilleshall.

Don Revie took over as full-time manager in the 1960/61 season, though early on their relationship was strained. He told Jack that he was prepared to let him go in 1962, but never actually transfer listed him. Liverpool manager Bill Shankly failed to meet the £30,000 Leeds demanded and though Manchester United manager Matt Busby was initially willing to pay the fee he decided against it. Jack signed a new contract with Leeds.

The 1962/63 season was the beginning of a new era for Leeds United as Don Revie began to mould the club into his own liking. In a game against Swansea City in September he played the young defensive line-up of Gary Sprake, Paul Reaney, Norman Hunter and Jack – to say they brought the best out of each other is to paraphrase history. Jack had his ideas about the defence formulation which Don Revie agreed with and the others supported – it paid off. Add Johnny Giles new in from Manchester United and other youngsters coming through like Billy Bremner, Paul Madeley and Peter Lorimer; Don Revie's masterpiece of a team were taking shape.

By 1964/65 Leeds were doing well but their reputation suffered. Jack said, 'The way we achieved that success made me feel uncomfortable'. They had a run of twenty-five games unbeaten and built up a rivalry with Manchester United. Leeds needed a win in their final game of the season to win the title but could only manage a three-all draw with Birmingham City at St Andrew's. Leeds also made it to the FA Cup final but were defeated by Liverpool.

They were second to Liverpool in the league the following season, and reached the semi-finals of the Inter-

City Fairs Cup; it was progress, but they had no trophies to show for it. There were to be none in the following season either. But Jack was named Footballer of the Year at the end of the 1966/67 season.

He continued to develop the role of the defender, through going up for corner kicks to bolster attack – he'd stand very close to the goalkeeper to limit his field of activity. This proved successful. Jack collected a winners trophy (tankard not a medal) when Leeds won the Football League Cup and then a medal when they won the Inter-City Fairs Cup in the 1967/68 season.

They won the league in 1968/69, on securing the title at Liverpool, Bill Shankly went into the Leeds dressing room after the match to tell them they were 'worthy champions'.

'People say Leeds United should have won a lot more – and maybe we would have won a lot more, if we hadn't been involved in every competition right until the end of each season. I mean, we got used to losing things... Yes, there was a lot of disappointment – but there was a lot of pride too, pride and passion and discipline which kept the Leeds family together when we might have fallen apart.'

The 1969/70 season started with Leeds beating Manchester City in the Charity Shield. Then came the realistic possibility of winning the treble – the league, FA Cup and European Cup, but they won neither, as a backlog of games built up the league title was the first to slip out of their hands; then the European Cup to Celtic (the crowd at Hampden Park was 136,505). After two replays in the FA Cup semis they beat Manchester United, but lost two-one in the replayed final to Chelsea. Jack lost concentration in the replay trying to retaliate from a kick, Peter Osgood enjoyed the remission and scored the equaliser.

He was quoted to have said he'd once had a 'little black book' of names of players whom he intended to hurt or exact some form of revenge upon during his playing days. He was tried by the FA and was found not guilty of any wrongdoing, arguing that the press had misquoted him. He did say there were a few players who had made nasty tackles on him and that he intended to put in a hard but fair challenge if he got the opportunity.

Leeds ended the season of 1970/71 in second place yet again, as Arsenal overtook them with a late series of one-nil wins, despite Leeds beating Arsenal in the penultimate game of the season after Jack scored the winner. The final tally of sixty-four points was a record high for a second-placed team. In the last season of the Inter-City Fairs Cup they beat Sarpsborg FK (Norway), Dynamo Dresden (West Germany), Sparta Prague (Czechoslovakia), Vitória (Portugal) and then Liverpool to play Juventus in the final. They drew two-all in Italy and one-all at Elland Road, but won on the away goals rule. They could have won the cup permanently, but lost by two goals to one to Barcelona in the trophy play-off game.

Leeds finished second again in the 1971/72 season, just one point behind Derby County. But they beat Arsenal by a goal to nil in the FA Cup final thanks to a superb Alan Clarke header.

Jack made only twenty-five appearances in the 1972/73 campaign and announced his retirement.

When he was getting to the end of his twenties, Jack was called up by Alf Ramsey for England in the two-all draw against Scotland in April 1965. He tasted defeat against Austria in October but was only defeated in an England shirt once more against Scotland in April 1967 – both games at Wembley.

England started 1966 with a one-all draw with Poland at Goodison Park on 5 January; Alf Ramsey allowed Bobby Moore to go forward to see if Jack and the full backs were okay – they were, and Bobby scored! The defensive line-up was juggled around a bit with Ron Flowers coming in for Jack and Norman Hunter coming in on a separate occasion for Bobby Moore, but otherwise Jack and Bobby were solid at the back throughout the World Cup victory and well after.

In the 1966 World Cup finals Jack ventured into forward positions periodically; in the second group game against France he hit the post with a header and Roger Hunt was there to clear up. It was in the semi-final against Portugal that Jack had the game of a lifetime – and he was not the only player on the pitch to do that either: he out-classed José Torres in the air, but made a perfect save with his hand late on for the penalty Eusabio converted from the spot.

In the final West Germany were helped into the lead. Jack felt that he could have blocked Helmut Haller's shot but thought Gordon Banks had it covered. England came back and then took the lead, but with only a few seconds left he had a free-kick awarded against him and after a goal-mouth scramble, Wolfgang Weber scored the equaliser. Geoff Hurst scored two goals in extra-time to win the game four-two.

After the World Cup, Brian Labone of Everton found himself in the England No. 5 shirt more frequently as Jack was either on duty for Leeds, or nursing an injury. Jack was in the squad for the European Championships in 1968, but didn't play. He won five caps in 1969, helping England to a memorable five-nil win over France and scoring in a one goal to nil win over Portugal from a corner taken by his brother Bobby.

He was in the squad of twenty-two for the 1970 World Cup in Mexico and picked up his thirty-fifth and final cap in the one-nil win over Czechoslovakia. On the flight home, Jack spoke to Alf Ramsey and felt he had given his all for England.

Jack moved into management and was offered the job as manager of Second Division Middlesbrough in 1973. He declined to be interviewed but listed responsibilities he expected to take, which if agreed, would give him total control of the running of the club. He decided to first repaint Ayresome Park and to publicise the upcoming league campaign to attract more supporters. He signed Bobby Murdoch on a free transfer from Celtic, and the club already had ten players which he could build with: Jim Platt (goalkeeper), John Craggs (right back), Stuart Boam and Willie Maddren (centre-backs), Frank Spraggon (left back), David Armstrong (left midfield), Graeme Souness (central midfield), Alan Foggon (attacking midfield), John Hickton and David Mills (forwards). He made Graeme Souness a more central player and encouraged him to play the ball forward rather than side to side. Alan Foggon was instructed to run in behind the opposing defence to beat any off-side trap: Alan was fast and the intention was to create a one-to-one on goalkeepers. Middlesbrough won promotion with seven games in hand at the end of the 1973/74 season. Jack wanted them to win the points to make them champions at home in front of their own crowd, but instinct took over and they beat Luton Town at Kenilworth Road. They were fifteen points ahead, and only fifteen points then covered third place with the relegation zone. Jack was made Manager of the Year, the title going out of the First Division for the very first time.

Jack was pleased to sign Terry Cooper at the beginning of the 1974/75 season, and Middlesbrough finished seventh in the First Division, falling three places in the last few minutes of the last match of the season!

In the 1975/76 season, they finished in thirteenth place, won the Anglo-Scottish Cup and reached the semi-finals of the Football League Cup. The following year they were about the same and Jack wondered if he had gone as far as he could with that group of players. Later he thought that he could have led the club to a league title if he had stayed and signed two more top quality players. He applied for the job of England manager after Don Revie quit the role but didn't receive a reply to his application.

In October 1977, he became manager at Sheffield Wednesday, then bottom of the Third Division, naming Maurice Setters as assistant. They both agreed that the football was poor in the division, but work rates were good. They advocated a kick-and-run tactic, pumping long and high passes – Jack bolstered his defence with taller players to prevent the opposition doing the same. Andrew McCulloch arrived in Yorkshire to form a partnership up front with Terry Curran. Big Mick Pickering arrived from Southampton and Bob Bolder, a goalkeeper, was also tall. It kept them safe with a fourteenth place finish at the end of the 1977/78 season.

Wednesday went on to secure promotion with a third-place finish, and Terry Curran finished as the division's top-scorer.

The 1980/81 season saw Wednesday comfortable in the Second Division, finishing tenth. They pushed for promotion the following season but ended just one place and one point outside the promotion places; disadvantaged by the new three point win system.

For the 1982/83 season he signed defender Mick Lyons from Everton. By Christmas Wednesday were top of the table, but with a limited squad, successful cup runs and injuries took their toll: they finished sixth. In the FA Cup semis they lost to Brighton. Jack announced his departure from Hillsborough in May 1983.

In March 1984, Malcolm Allison left Middlesbrough and Jack took temporary charge until the end of the season. They managed to stay seven points clear of the relegation zone.

Jack was appointed manager of Newcastle United in June 1984 after being persuaded to take the job by Jackie Milburn. Kevin Keegan announced his retirement, and Terry McDermott hadn't agreed a new contract. Jack had little money to spend in preparation for the 1984/85 season but there were young talents in Chris Waddle and Peter Beardsley. He signed Gary Megson and striker George Reilly, and a teenaged Paul Gascoigne was coming through the youth system. Jack left early in the 1985/86 season.

He was approached to manage the Republic of Ireland national team in December 1985. The following May, Ireland won the Iceland Triangular Tournament, with a two-one victory over their hosts and a one-nil win over Czechoslovakia. Jack had adopted the British four-four-two system, as most of his players were with English clubs. He instructed members of his team to pressure opposition players and in particular force defenders into mistakes.

Qualification for Euro 1988 meant winning a group containing Bulgaria, Luxembourg and Scotland. They started with a two-all draw with Belgium; Frank Stapleton and Liam Brady scored the goals. Ireland dominated Scotland at Lansdowne Road in Dublin, but both sides failed to score. In the return fixture at Hampden Park they won by a goal to nil. They faltered with a two goals to one defeat in Bulgaria, though Jack felt that neither of Bulgaria's goals should have been allowed: Mick McCarthy was pushed in the build-up to the first, and after a foul by Kevin Moran the referee gave a penalty when the infringement was clearly outside the eighteen-yard box. They picked up another point after a nil-nil draw with Belgium in Dublin. Ireland then had two victories over Luxembourg and a home win over Bulgaria, The Irish had to rely on the Scots to qualify, who obliged with a goal to nil victory in Sofia.

'Every player we brought into the squad considered himself Irish... Had it not been for the economic circumstances which forced their parents or grandparents to emigrate, they would have been born and reared in Ireland. Should they now be victimized and denied their heritage because of the whims of journalists? I think not.'

The build-up to Euro 1988 in West Germany was far from ideal, as three key players were injured. Their first match was against England and Jack thought that the threat posed by English wingers Chris Waddle and John Barnes could be contained by closing down passes out to them; this made any build up to an attack slow and manageable. It worked and Ireland won by a goal to nil. They drew with the Soviet Union despite injury problems, but with Ronnie Whelan and Kevin Sheedy in central midfield, the game saw a solid performance. To qualify they only needed a point against the Netherlands, but they lost by a goal to nil.

In the 1990 World Cup they shared a group with Spain, Hungary, Northern Ireland and Malta. Ireland started with a goalless draw with Northern Ireland; then Spain beat them two-nil. They dominated the fixture in Hungary but dropped a point. Their final four fixtures were played in Dublin, and they qualified for their first World Cup finals in Italy.

Ireland's group opponents in Italia '90 were England, Egypt and the Netherlands. Jack felt that England's four-man midfield didn't offer enough protection to the back four, and he was proved right when Kevin Sheedy cancelled out Gary Lineker's goal for a one-all draw. But a poor performance against the Egyptians earned them only the one point. They had another draw with the Netherlands which meant that both qualified. Ireland then defeated Romania on penalties in the second round after yet another draw, before the whole team had a meeting with Pope John Paul II at the Vatican. Ireland went on to meet Italy in the quarter-finals but lost by a goal to nil: Italy's Salvatore Schillaci scored in the thirty-eighth minute. In Dublin over 500,000 people turned out to welcome the team back.

For Euro '92 in Sweden, Ireland faced a group of England, Poland and Turkey. They opened in style with a five-nil home win over the Turks and then drew one-all home and away to England. Ireland were the better team in both encounters; Jack said they 'twice let them off the hook'. A no-score draw at home with Poland followed, and they were then leading by three goals to one in the return fixture in Poznań but conceded two late goals to end the match at three goals each. Ireland beat Turkey three-one in Istanbul, but were denied a place in the tournament as England scored a late equalizing goal in Poland to finish above Ireland in the group.

To qualify for the 1994 World Cup in the United States, Ireland had to finish first or second in a seven team group of Spain, Denmark, Northern Ireland, Lithuania, Latvia, and Albania. Lithuania, Latvia and Albania proved to be of little threat, and they secured the maximum two points from each game. The two most difficult fixtures – Denmark and Spain away – ended in goalless draws, and John Aldridge had a goal disallowed for offside against the Spanish. Ireland then beat Northern Ireland three-nil in Dublin before settling for a goal a piece draw with Denmark. In the opening twenty-six minutes of the match in Spain the hosts took a three goal lead; the game ended three-one, with John Sheridan's late consolation eventually proving crucial. The final game was in Belfast against Northern Ireland. Jimmy Quinn put Northern Ireland ahead on seventy-four minutes, but four minutes later Alan McLoughlin equalised to give the Republic of Ireland second place in the group due to their superior goal difference.

In the build-up to the World Cup first caps went to Gary Kelly, Phil Babb and Jason McAteer. Jack scheduled difficult matches before the tournament and Ireland picked up positive results by beating The Netherlands and West Germany away. They opened the group stage of the tournament by beating Italy by a goal to nil, thanks to a Ray Houghton strike. They suffered a two-one defeat to Mexico, during which Jack was involved in an argument with an official who was preventing substitute John Aldridge from taking the pitch. They faced the Netherlands in the next round; Dennis Bergkamp put the Dutch ahead and Wim Jonk scored the second from thirty yards.

Ireland failed to qualify for Euro '96 despite a strong start to the group, winning their first three games: one a four goals to nil win against Northern Ireland. Their next game was also against Northern Ireland, but finished one-all. From then on they had some injuries to key players. After beating the highly fancied Portugal, the Irish then endured a goalless draw to Liechtenstein – the tiny nation's only point in ten games – and lost twice to Austria. Although they defeated Latvia, Ireland needed to beat Portugal in Lisbon, but lost three-nil, and finished second in the group on goal difference. As the worst performing runners-up they had to win a play-off game at Anfield against the Netherlands; they lost by two goals to nil. Jack retired:

'In my heart of hearts, I knew I'd wrung as much as I could out of the squad I'd got – that some of my older players had given me all they had to give.'

He'd married Pat Kemp on 6 January 1958, and Bobby was best man. John junior was born in 1959, Deborah two years later and Peter in 1966. In the 1960s Jack ran outfitters shops in Leeds, and a souvenir shop at Elland Road. He is also noted as a keen amateur fisherman and also takes part in field sport.

He was awarded an OBE in 1974. In 1996 he was awarded honorary Irish citizenship, made a Freeman of the city of Dublin, and given an honorary doctorate by the University of Limerick.

Big Jack was inducted into the English Football Hall of Fame in 2005 in recognition of his contribution to the English game.

6

Bobby Moore – Defender: Left Half and Captain

Robert Frederick Moore was born on 12 April 1941 and died on 24 February 1993. From the 1966 squad only Les Cocker pre-deceased him; Bobby was the figurehead, the captain of the National Team and was Alf Ramsey's representative on the field. He was also one of the best players the country has produced, and Pele, of whom no one has the slightest doubt that he was the greatest, said Bobby was 'the greatest defender I ever played against.'

At club level he captained West Ham United for over a decade and lifted the FA Cup, and The European Cup Winners Cup – but the greatest moment in English football history must be his, when Her Majesty the Queen presented captain Bobby Moore with the Jules Rimet trophy, the World Cup.

He was the record holder, after Billy Wright and Bobby Charlton, of the total amount of caps won playing for England, at 108: he left the international scene in 1973, and stepped down from the First Division in 1974: but he wasn't finished yet because his new club Fulham nearly defeated West Ham in the FA Cup final in 1975.

Bobby played for the school teams at both Westbury Primary School and then later Tom Hood School in Leytonstone. And was soon ready to start on his upward journey through the youth team at West Ham United, who he joined in 1956. His first appearance for the first team came only two years later when Malcolm Allison – who'd previously occupied the No. 6 shirt at Upton Park – was out suffering from tuberculosis: sadly Malcolm never came back to the shirt, or the First Division, but did manage a few other things!

Bobby was always completely composed no matter at which level he was playing: which was enough on its own to stand him above many of his contemporaries. Gordon Banks said he was always well ahead in anticipating what a player would do, and Jock Stein suggested he was about twenty minutes ahead! So there was a great economy of effort – he didn't jump as heading wasn't his forte nor was he hard-tackling, indeed he often made taking the ball off a world class opponent look almost casual. I have read and heard that he wasn't a very fast mover but I'd refer to the opening goal in the 1966 World Cup final when Halmut Haller suddenly finds himself in possession in the eighteen-yard box – Bobby could have overtaken a bullet as he tried to get across to him.

It was only a couple of years after his club debut that the England manager Walter Winterbottom invited him to join the under-23 level squad but it seems he graduated without kicking a ball to the full England squad. The selection committee chose him for England's campaign in Chile in the 1962 World Cup finals and it was during England's warm-up tour that he made his international debut. This was in a four-nil win against Peru in May 1962. Maurice Norman also won his first cap that day and the defence looked comfortable, so the two of them stayed in the team for the whole tournament, with Pele and Brazil gaining victory in the quarter-finals.

But it was after the 1962/63 season when we'd all shivered with the weather and a backlog of fixtures built up, that Bobby took on the role of captain of England for the first time. His immediate predecessor Jimmy Armfield was injured – he'd been captain on fifteen occasions and Johnny Haynes had left the international scene after captaining for twenty-two matches. Ronnie Clayton took up the role a few times but Bobby was to equal Billy Wright in captaining his country for ninety matches! David Beckham, the most capped outfield player, took the role on for fifty-nine matches and the present incumbent, Steven Gerrard, has chalked up thirty-four. So if you think about the latter two being *real icons*, then where does that place Bobby Moore in the overall scheme of things – it's difficult if not impossible to say.

In Bobby's first match as captain England took on the very able Czechoslovakian side and beat them by four goals to two. Jimmy Armfield did come back to the role of captain but Bobby had shown his metal. Alf Ramsey had only recently been appointed and the Czech game was the first as permanently appointed manager, following his departure from Ipswich Town. A perfect partnership was in the making. Come the summer friendlies of 1964, Bobby came to be the first choice as captain for the national team.

And in 1964 he got his hands on the FA Cup when, as captain of West Ham United, they beat Preston North End in the FA Cup final by three goals to two: Ronnie Boyce headed home the winner just before time. Peter Brabrook and John Bond carried Bobby shoulder high with the cup.

He was the Football Writers' Association Footballer of the Year but cancer entered his life. However, first time around it was successfully treated.

In 1965 he went up the Wembley steps again courtesy of two goals by the late Alan Sealey to beat TSV 1860 Munchen in the European Cup Winners' Cup.

At this point in his career Bobby had completely matured and was Alf Ramsey's first choice as England captain – he was used to walking up the Wembley steps, and Alf had predicted England would win the World Cup in 1966. As part of the warm-up the England team went up to Goodison Park in Liverpool to take on a Polish side – and Bobby scored the goal in the one-all draw.

Back at club level West Ham were defeated by five goals to three in the then two-legged Football League Cup final by West Bromwich Albion. Again he had scored a goal in the first leg at Upton Park.

Up at international level once again, Bobby scored against Norway two weeks before the 1966 World Cup finals got underway in London.

West Ham United (and future England) manager Ron Greenwood and Bobby were summoned to a meeting with Alf Ramsey over a slight technicality – Bobby Moore's contract with West Ham United had lapsed and therefore he was ineligible to play for his country. I'm not sure whether there had been a problem with Bobby and West Ham or it was just an administrative error, but Alf probably slept a lot better that night after that detail had been tidied up.

In the final tournament Bobby played and was captain in all the matches, both in the group section as well as the knock-out stage. A lot has been made of his lack of pace – but speed isn't always an accurate qualitative measure, and if another player could 'get there quicker' one has to ask if the outcome would be any better. Alf was reputed to have questioned if Bobby was fast enough for the West Germans and whether Norman Hunter would be better suited to defend alongside his Leeds teammate, Jack Charlton. In the finish this didn't happen and Alf was overheard discussing it in what might have been a much longer discussion about the entire team. He was under pressure to drop Nobby Stiles and also return Jimmy Greaves to the front line, so perhaps Alf questioned his selection of the entire eleven.

It is possible that team understandings came into the Norman or Bobby equation but it was Bobby Moore who propelled the ball onto Geoff Hurst's head for the equaliser and helped the ball onto his teammates left foot for the forth goal. The equaliser came after a free kick had been awarded and Bobby was very quick in launching the ball to exactly where he knew Geoff would travel to.

It was Bobby who had the best view of the ball hitting Karl-Heinz Schnellinger following Lothar Emmerich's free-kick in the last few seconds of the final, and he appealed for hand ball: it wasn't. Bobby had to rally the men for extra time. Alf said he thought the West German side were exhausted.

The pass Bobby made in the final few seconds of extra time was perfect – it would have been a shame if the final was decided on Geoff Hurst's second, England's third; the most controversial goal of the tournament. But at four goals to two, England were winners. And winning the game brought about a further worry for Bobby as he had to shake hands with the Queen when the trophy was presented, so he wiped his hands on the velvet table a few seconds before the presentation.

It would be difficult to find anyone who was surprised to see Bobby Moore awarded with the BBC's Sports Personality of the Year in 1966, and he was in royal circles again when collecting an OBE in the New Year's Honours list.

His fiftieth cap for England came when England beat Wales at Wembley in November 1966, a match that was actually for England to qualify for the 1968 European Championships. In this tournament he led them again but they finished third.

England qualified for the 1970 World Cup finals as holders, so Alf could juggle the team around in the series of friendlies England played prior to the tournament – players needed to get used to the differing climate. The entire episode of the pre-tournament tour in South America was to turn very ugly for Bobby.

There were two warm-up matches in Central America, Columbia and Equador. On 20 May 1970 England beat Columbia by four goals to nil in a thoroughly professional way. Four days later it was the turn of Ecuador, by two goals to nil. However Bobby Charlton thought about buying a piece of jewellery for his wife, so at the squad's hotel in Bogata he had a look in a jewellery shop. Bobby Moore was with him and one cannot imagine a more gentlemanly pair. But the allegation was made against Bobby Moore that he stole a bracelet valued at £600 and even though he himself knew he was completely innocent, as subsequently proved, it unnerved the squad. He travelled a bit later to Equador as he was placed under 'house arrest' but won his eightieth cap in a two goals to nil victory. When the squad returned to Columbia, Bobby was arrested on touch-down. The magistrate, though, threw the case out when one of the witnesses changed their mind about which jacket pocket they said they saw him put the bracelet in, and another witness withdrew their statement. Bobby and the team eventually arrived in Mexico and Bobby announced that the only thing on his mind was winning the World Cup.

The familiar No. 6 shirt saw four games. In the opening game against Romania he showed that he'd put the entire episode in Columbia behind him. Against Brazil, even in defeat, it has been said this was his best ever game. One tackle against Jairzinho was so well timed and executed the whole world gasped. Gordon Banks and Bobby had a short discussion after what has been described as the best save ever made in first class football – apparently Bob muttered something about giving away a corner. The game ended with Brazil winning by the single goal but it was the best match of the tournament, and the picture of Bobby and Pele at the end of the game is the epitome of sportsmanship and racial harmony.

The final group game saw Alan Clark (on his England debut) convert a penalty to see England progress to the next round. Against West Germany all went well initially, but whereas at Wembley in 1966 England had maintained their strength as the West Germans weakened, in Mexico it was the other way around as England's two goal lead was whittled down, equalled and then Gerd Muller got the winner in extra time. England were no longer World Champions. And Gerd Muller just pipped Bobby again later that year as he was announced European Footballer of the Year.

But Bobby had lifted the Jules Rimet trophy, which no one else in an England shirt had ever done. Actually, that year Brazil won the tournament for a third time, so they kept the old trophy permanently. (No English captain has yet to receive the new cup.)

In early August a threat to kidnap Bobby's wife made him pull out of West Ham United's pre-season friendly fixtures, but in the event Mrs Moore remained safe.

In February 1973 Bobby won his one hundredth international cap when England beat Scotland by five goals to nil at Hampden Park, and he hadn't long taken his club total to over five hundred. In 1973 only Alan Ball and Martin Peters with Bobby were still on the international scene – some players who had moved away from the three lions shirt or had been sent packing by Alf Ramsey were younger: he was to make more appearances, he wasn't finished yet.

However, now he was in his thirties he wasn't as sharp as he had been, and opposition strikers were getting quicker. In a qualifying match for the 1974 World Cup, Poland had a very strong side and in the away match in Chorzów he got in the way of a free kick which, from the deflection, sailed into Peter Shilton's goal. He was later dispossessed by Wlodzimierz Lubanski, who got Poland's second goal – he was five years Bobby's junior and a real star striker – so the best might have been said to beat the best in that match. It has been said that Alf dropped him, which isn't true as he played in the following two internationals, but Norman Hunter, who'd waited patiently for that No. 6 shirt, was brought in for a win against Austria and a month later Norman stayed there for the return match with Poland at Wembley. The Polish goalkeeper Jan Tomaszewski was magnificent and saved everything thrown at him. Poland qualified.

Bobby's final international for England was against Italy at Wembley on 4 November 1973, which ended in a one-nil defeat. But when he went to America he was 'capped' for a bicentennial match against England. That day he pumped the ball into the box for Pele who was capped as an American player!

The draw with Poland could be said to mark the end of Alf Ramsey's pre-eminence as England manager and by some irony the only subsequent England manager to get anywhere near close to Alf in public standing was another Ipswich Town old boy, Bobby Robson.

But in the second Poland match Bobby Moore reflected: 'I said to Alf we need someone to go through the middle. He just nodded. We couldn't get Kevin (Hector) out there quick enough. We almost threw him onto the pitch.'

So Bobby's international career was dazzling to say the least: he'd beaten Billy Wright's record of 105 caps and equalled his record of matches as captain – ninety. He has to be considered as one of the finest players ever to grace an England shirt, and although latterly David Beckham has passed his record and Steve Gerrard looks set to pass it also, it doesn't look likely that his legacy for club and country will be beaten just yet.

In January 1974 he sustained a rare injury in a game against Hereford United in the FA Cup – in his 544th appearance for West Ham and sadly his last.

He moved across London to Fulham who were then in the Second Division and £25,000 went the other way. But Bobby wasn't finished with West Ham – though Fulham were defeated in the Football League Cup by them. At Wembley on 3 May 1975, along with Alan Mullery, Fulham lined up against West Ham United in the FA Cup final. And they did well, but two Alan Taylor goals saw the trophy go back to Upton Park where Bobby had taken it just over a decade before. On the day he looked as sharp as ever: Billy Bonds was by then West Ham Captain and it was he who topped Bobby's record of appearances with the club.

In total Bobby played for the Craven Cottage-based Fulham on 124 occasions, the final game being against Blackburn Rovers at Ewood Park in May 1977 – the final score was a one-nil defeat for Fulham.

Like many of his generation he travelled across the Atlantic and showed the Americans how it was done. He played twenty-four games for San Antonio Thunder and made seven appearances for Seattle Sounders. In April 1978 he signed for the Danish club Herning Fremad and played nine games to help push the Danes into professional football.

In management his career never really got off the ground. He looked after the Hong Kong side Eastern AA before brief spells with Oxford City and Southend United. His assistant at Oxford City was his old West Ham team mate Harry Rednapp.

At Southend United, Bobby was on the board. When former Norwich City star Peter Morris left the club, Bobby took over as manager, but a local businessman Anton Johnson was accused of all sorts of irregularities and if mud sticks it can also splash. The club lost a lot of money and questions were asked about this too, but on the field Southend didn't set the world alight. After a couple of lacklustre seasons when they finished low in the Fourth Division they started to put a few results together and eventually finished ninth in the 1985/86 season.

Frank Lampard (senior) joined Bobby and things were looking up, at any rate on the pitch. But Bobby wanted out; former Chelsea FA Cup winner David Webb took over and continued what Bobby had started – within a couple of seasons promotion came along. He could have built on this but may not have got the opportunity. There were some businesses he was involved in which didn't take him anywhere and it left the question as to why the FA didn't find him a role as the only English player to captain the World Champions.

He did join Capital Gold, a London radio station, in 1990 so he was still involved in the game.

It must have been with some sadness that Bobby and Tina Moore parted in 1986 after twenty odd years of marriage – but Bobby found happiness again with Stephanie by the time they married in December 1991. Bobby's health wasn't great and he'd fought cancer before – he had what was referred to as an 'emergency' stomach operation in April 1991, and a lot of people were holding their breath.

But the inevitable happened or, one should say, the expected because after a lot of conjecture Bobby publically announced he had cancer in early February 1993 and by this time the cancer had spread to other parts of his body. He was aged just fifty-one when he passed away in the early morning of 24 February 1993.

His mother Doris had died just the year before: his father, also Robert, had passed away in 1978. Bobby was cremated at the City of London Cemetery and Crematorium and his ashes were buried with his parents.

His departure from Upton Park had not been a particularly happy one and there followed an absence of some years after he was refused entry. But that was high-flying football politics. When it come to the fans – the people who really matter – there was almost a tidal wave of flowers and tributes. On 6 March 1993 Wolverhampton Wanderers played West Ham United at Upton Park and the whole ground was a sea of flowers, scarves and other tributes. Geoff Hurst with Martin Peters placed a floral creation of Bobby's No. 6 shirt in the centre circle. Ian Bishop, the then wearer of the shirt, wore No. 12 for the game. West Ham won, but all of football throughout the world had lost.

There followed a memorial service at Westminster Abbey in late June, attended by all of the 1966 squad. Such a service was a rarity for a sportsman and he was the first footballer to be honoured in that way. The Dean of Westminster was quoted to have said:

'For many years he delighted supporters of West Ham and was a formidable opponent in the eyes of those against whom he played. But it is for his appearances for England — ninety of them as captain — that he will be chiefly remembered, and supremely for his captaincy of the World Cup team of 1966.'

Stephanie Moore set up a charity The Bobby Moore Fund to raise money for research into bowel cancer and to raise awareness. George Cohen also had the disease. It is treatable and some of the symptoms are noticeable, but if a surgeon can do a straightforward colonoscopy then the disease can be caught early and the outcome is very likely to be favourable: a colonoscopy takes only a short while and the patient is sedated. It needs to be done every two years in folk who are over fifty, with a family history of the disease. The Bobby Moore fund has raised millions of pounds and one hopes it has helped lessen the mortality of the disease.

A stand at Upton Park was named The Bobby Moore Stand and in August 2008 West Ham United officially retired the No. 6 shirt as a mark of respect.

Bobby was selected as the Golden Player of England by the FA which conveys their feeling – shared by many – that he was the outstanding player of the past 50 years.

Wembley Stadium was redeveloped in the new millennium, and when rebuilt the finishing touch was a statue of Bob, unveiled in May 2007 by Sir Bobby Charlton (Bobby Moore would almost certainly have been knighted too had he lived). Bobby Moore stands proud with his foot on a ball looking along Wembley Way.

'My captain, my leader, my right-hand man. He was the spirit and the heartbeat of the team. A cool, calculating footballer I could trust with my life. He was the supreme professional, the best I ever worked with. Without him England would never have won the World Cup,' said Alf Ramsey.

'Moore was the best defender I have ever seen.' Sir Alex Ferguson

'He knows what's happening 20 minutes before everyone else.' Jock Stein.

Even a book about the highlights of his career would be huge, from saving a penalty while he temporarily stood in goal for West Ham against Stoke City in 1972, to making a tackle against one the world's greatest players Jairzinho in Mexico in 1970. Not only was he a brilliant soccer player, but a talented cricketer and he played for the Essex Youth Team, together with Geoff Hurst! He also stared in a Hollywood blockbuster alongside Pele, Mike Summerbee (Bobby got him involved) and other icons aided and abetted by Michael Caine and Sylvestor Stallone: *Escape to Victory*.

He was in every sense an icon but what a shame his football effectively ended in 1977 when he could have offered so much as a national representative – one commentator suggested that as Bobby was so great and the England sides of the Seventies were not quite as successful (which had a lot to do with luck – or lack of it) he became an unwelcome a reminder of the embarrassment that the game was in the late Seventies. But the Team of '66 was lucky to have Bobby Moore as the captain of the national team in the national sport.

He had two children with Tina in the 1960s: Roberta was born in early 1965 and son Dean in the late spring of 1968 – Dean was Tina's maiden name. Sadly Dean died in 2011.

7

Alan Ball – Midfielder: Attack

Alan James Ball, at twenty-one, was the youngest in the 1966 squad.

He played for a number of clubs and also managed some of them in later years. Alan lost his father to a road crash in 1982 – his father had also been a professional footballer and manager. And Alan's wife also passed away only a few shades after her youth in May 2004 after a long battle with ovarian cancer.

Alan played a total of 833 competitive games at club level and won seventy-two caps for England. In his twenty-two year career he scored nearly two hundred goals, and for a time was the most expensive footballer in the country.

He began at Blackpool whilst still a schoolboy, playing for Ashton United, the team his father managed. Alan eventually came to prominence at Blackpool. He had had a youth contract at Wolverhampton Wanderers, but after he left school, Wolves decided not to take him on. He started training with Bolton Wanderers but they thought he was too small and didn't give him a professional deal. Eventually Blackpool signed him after his father pulled a few strings. Alan was given a trial in September 1961 and signed up as an apprentice, turning professional in May 1962. His debut was away against Liverpool on 18 August 1962; Blackpool won two-one. At age 17 years and 98 days he was the youngest league player to grace Bloomfield Road.

All eyes were on the England team throughout the 1966 World Cup finals and Alan in particular attracted a lot of interest; just a couple of months after the World Cup, Everton came along and he signed for them for £112,000. That completed the best midfield club trio in the country: Alan Ball, Colin Harvey and Howard Kendall. Everton had a bit of bad luck insofar as they reached the FA Cup final in 1968 only to be beaten by a Jeff Astle goal for West Bromwich Albion. The following year Manchester City knocked them out in the semis – City went on to win the cup. But Everton took the League Championship in 1970, just staying ahead of the mighty Leeds United.

In December 1971, Bertie Mee of Arsenal paid a fee of £220,000 to take him to London. By this time Alan was twenty-six and at his peak. He made his debut the day after Boxing Day at Nottingham Forest where the points were shared and the result was a goal a-piece. Alan described his debut as 'adequate' which wasn't echoed by the fans on his home debut against Everton on New Years Day 1972. He had to wait until the 15 January 1972 for his first goal, which came in the sixty-eighth minute away to Swindon Town in the FA Cup.

He became a regular in the Highbury team, chalking up 50 appearances in the 1972/73 season, and scoring ten goals in the league. But the double-winning side had gradually wound down and changed, and some of their replacements didn't quite seem to gel. Alan became club captain in 1974 but was out for a good while after he broke his leg, so was not in the side for the start of the 1974/75 season. Arsenal had slipped to the lower part of the First Division and at the beginning of the 1975/76 season he was, again, injured. The management structure at Arsenal changed and former player Terry Neill took up the reins. In December 1976 after five years at Highbury, Alan was transferred to Southampton for the more modest fee of £60,000.

His skill, tenacity and experience saw Southampton rise to the First Division again and be runners-up in the Football League Cup in 1979. From his base at The Dell he made 132 appearances and scored nine goals.

Then came the North American Soccer League (NASL) – Alan was with Philidelphia Fury, where he was also for a time player/coach, before playing for Vancouver Whitecaps. But he returned to Blackpool as player/manager from the winter of 1980. He was back at Bloomfield Road for a year but it turned out the role was far more difficult than he thought it would be, and at the beginning of the 1980/81 season Blackpool were struggling. His relationship with the fans was also strained and he was critical of their support. On 28 February 1981 Blackpool were beaten by Brentford by two goals to nil and looking stranded three points adrift and second from bottom of the Third Division – they were eventually relegated. Alan was dismissed.

But it didn't take him long to bounce back, and in boots too. He returned to Southampton and played with old England mates Mike Channon and Kevin Keegan, racking up another sixty-three appearances before he went east to Australia and Hong Kong.

After a brief final spell at Bristol Rovers, Alan hung up his boots after a long and incredibly distinguished club career where he notched up 975 games.

His international career had finished on a bit of a sad note. Leslie Ball, his wife picked, up the phone one day in late summer of 1975 and was asked how Alan felt about being dropped by new national manager Don Revie. It was a bad public relations clanger to drop: Alan had only been out because of injury.

It was for ten years that he'd played for England after making his debut on 9 May 1965 in a one-all draw with Yugoslavia, when he hadn't even reached his twentieth birthday! His third cap was just a week later in Gothenburg when he scored his first international goal. Alf Ramsey was trying to capitalise on midfield and use full backs to overlap, which could see the side reverting to the defensive a lot easier. Over the next year England played twelve fixtures and Alan played in just over half but this was Alf experimenting and fine-tuning to deliver on his promise that England would win the World Cup in 1966.

Alan was the youngest in a squad of twenty-two for the tournament. Three comparatively inexperienced international players stamped their mark on the world: Alan, Martin Peters and Geoff Hurst. It would be interesting to know just how much ground Alan covered in that No. 7 shirt as he never stopped running from the first whistle to trying to hold Geoff up after the fourth goal went in right at the end of extra time in the final.

Strange to consider that at that time, this star of the English game still lived with his parents and sister!

Alan's collection of caps mounted as the seasons rolled round and in the next World Cup game England played, in Mexico against Romania, he made his forty-second appearance. That tournament gave a lot of amazing moments but curiously the game against Brazil may have had a different outcome – Alan hit the bar – what if he'd scored? And as Tostao started his jiggle to pass to Pele to pass to Jairzinho to score, he elbowed Alan in the face and the ref should have blown. On form England were a match for Brazil, who annihilated Italy, who beat West Germany. But England's luck had ran out.

In the run-up to the 1974 finals things got worse. A scuffle with the Polish midfielder Lesław Ćmikiewicz prompted the ref to show Alan a red card and invite him to leave the field. Poland qualified for the finals – where they did well – and England failed to qualify. It was to be a watershed period for the English national team.

Alan didn't play for England under Joe Mercer's short caretaker tenure but under Don Revie, to start with at any rate, it couldn't have been better. Alan was appointed captain and led a team that didn't lose a game: they convincingly beat the then World Champions, West Germany and demolished the auld enemy Scotland by five goals to one. A later injury meant Don Revie forgot him, permanently. At thirty and after seventy-two appearances, he'd played his last for England.

He still performed well back at club level but with mixed results as player/manager. When Alan took up his managerial career in May 1984, landing the Portsmouth job, it was a big success. But like success stories in soccer, club chairmen tend to get in the way. However Alan just missed out on promotion for his first two seasons but did take Portsmouth up in 1987. But they only lasted one season before coming down again – in January 1989 he was sacked.

He didn't have to wait long for his next pay cheque. He joined Colchester United as assistant to Jock Wallace and in October 1989 took up a similar post under Mick Mills at Stoke City. Mick was sacked quite soon afterwards and Alan was put in charge. He let six of the squad go and brought six new players in. It was a huge gamble and it didn't pay off. Stoke remained at the bottom of the Second Division and were ultimate relegated.

Stoke wanted an instant return to the Second Division and it looked an attainable goal, because with twelve games played in 1990/91 they were one of the favourites for promotion. Form fell off, though, and they lost some games with some unfortunate score-lines, slipping down the table. When they got beaten four-nil at Wigan, Alan was instructed to vacate the manager's office.

He joined Exeter City, who were in the Third Division, as manager in July 1991. Exeter struggled and were strapped for cash but he managed to keep them in what became the Second Division when the Premier League was created.

Alan worked alongside Graham Taylor the England Manager from February to August 1992, which covered the 1992 European Championships in Sweden, but they were not a success as England failed to progress beyond the group stages.

He returned to Southampton in January 1994, and they seemed doomed to relegation: they had spent virtually the whole season in danger of relegation. Alan re-established Matt Le Tissier's role in the team, a player he considered was the club's greatest asset. Matt started scoring goals: six in the next four games, including a hat-trick on 14 February 1994 in a four-two victory over Liverpool. In the second half of the 1993/94 season, Matt made sixteen appearances and scored fifteen goals. But Southampton suffered three defeats over the Easter period and were still in the relegation zone. In their final six games that season their form improved, and they scored fifteen goals, Matt scored eight, which won them ten points. Their safety was confirmed on the final day of the season.

A good signing for Alan at the beginning of the 1994/95 season was the Liverpool goalkeeper Bruce Grobbelaar and Matt Le Tissier signed a new three-year contract. But Southampton took no points at all from their first four games and it seemed Alan had problems in defence as well as in attack. One result that went against them was a five-one hammering at Newcastle United. The Danish striker Ronnie Ekelund came to the Dell on loan and in September they won four games out of five to climb up to sixth in the Premiership. But the improvement wasn't maintained and they slipped up more than they ran. They hovered around the relegation zone, but there was one amazing match which summed up Southampton's topsy-turvy season: on 22 March a crowd of 14,666 saw Paul Kitson put Newcastle United ahead at the Dell with a spectacular goal and the match turned dreary – try as he might, Alan couldn't motivate his team until Neil Heaney gently tapped in to equalise after Pavel Srnicek made a good save from Jim Magilton, who didn't hold the ball. The goalkeeper didn't earn himself any more favours a minute later when Gordon Watson put Southampton ahead on his debut for the club before Neil Shipperley made it three-one. This result inspired Southampton, who won five of their remaining games to finish the season in a respectable tenth place.

But Alan resigned to take over at Manchester City and it did not go down too well with the crowd at the Dell. For some years afterwards his visits were greeted by abuse from sections of the Southampton faithful. Alan's tenure at Maine Road was controversial in that many observers and supporters felt he was appointed for his name and friendship with the chairman rather than for any credentials as a coach.

Alan paid cash plus Paul Walsh, who'd scored fifteen league and cup goals for City in 1994/95, to Portsmouth in exchange for Gerry Creaney. But Manchester City made a dreadful start to the 1995/96 season, experiencing eight defeats and three draws at the start of the campaign, and when they were defeated by six goals to nil by Liverpool, they prayed for a miracle. But November saw a turnaround in fortunes when Alan's men finally managed to win a league game: a Summerbee scored in the next match as Mike's son Nicky took the points at Maine Road to beat Bolton Wanderers by a goal to nil. They were then unbeaten throughout November and Alan was named manager of the month. The return match with Liverpool was their last of the season but they were, in fact, relegated. Alan resigned.

In February 1998 he was re-appointed as Portsmouth Manager. The club was to be taken over and the would-be new owner wanted Alan to manage the club, but the sale didn't go through. They were left in financial difficulties and in the relegation zone. Alan led the club to survival, as two of his former clubs – Stoke City and Manchester City – went down to the Second Division. Portsmouth finished twentieth with the same goal difference as Queens Park Rangers, but their survival wasn't secured until the last match of the season when they won three-one at Bradford City. Things were looking up in the club's financial status but they were in the lower half of the First Division by the mid-season of 1998/99. His contract was terminated.

With Jack Charlton, Alan was the only member of the 1966 winning team to have survived football management.

In 2000 he was awarded the MBE as a member of the squad from the 1966 final. Three years later he was inducted into the English Football Hall of Fame.

He also entered the Hall of Fame at Bloomfield Road, when it was officially opened by former Blackpool player Jimmy Armfield in April 2006. Organised by the Blackpool Supporters' Association, Blackpool fans around the world voted on their all-time heroes. Five players from each decade are inducted and Alan represents the 1960s.

He was already in Everton's Hall of Fame and for the start of the 2003/04 season, as part of the club's official celebration of their 125th anniversary, Alan was voted by the supporters as a member of Everton's best ever team.

He more-or-less retired and within a couple of years his wife, Lesley was diagnosed, only on a routine check, with ovarian cancer. Sadly the disease took its toll and she passed away in May 2004. Their daughter also faced a cancer battle, but that seems to have cleared up.

Alan and Lesley had married in late spring of 1967. They had three children, Mandy (Miranda) in spring 1968, Keely three years later and James in late 1975. There are also grandchildren.

Alan and Lesley had remained in touch with some of their very early friends, one of whom, Valerie became close to Alan after Lesley's passing.

Valerie had been to see Alan at his house in Hampshire and she thought it pleasant that he'd waved goodbye far longer than usual, though in a way she thought odd. Later

1. Alf Ramsey ahead of Bobby Moore leads England out for the opening match in the 1966 finals against Uruguay: the result was nil-nil.

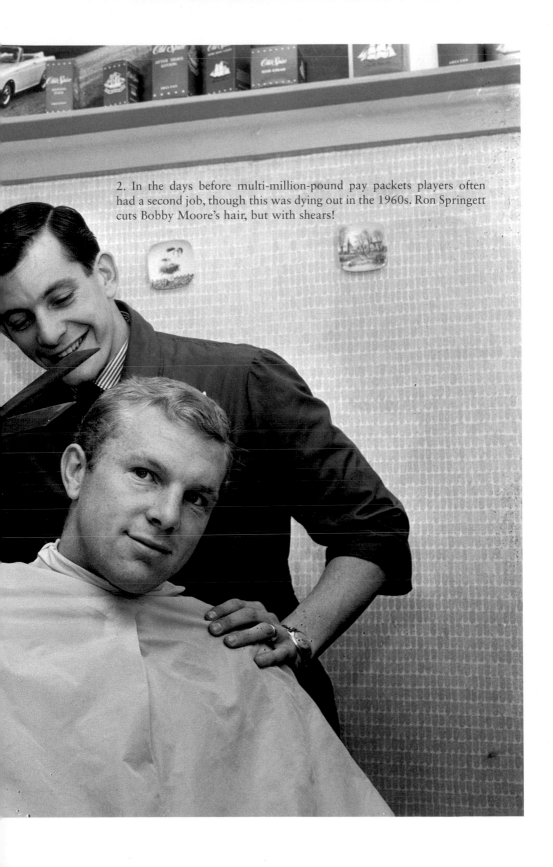

2. In the days before multi-million-pound pay packets players often had a second job, though this was dying out in the 1960s. Ron Springett cuts Bobby Moore's hair, but with shears!

3. Back to the day job. In August 1966 Fulham played host to Everton. Alan Ball (left) freshly in from Blackpool scored the only goal of the game. George Cohen (centre) and Ray Wilson (right) let him have the limelight.

4. February 1966 at Wembley against West Germany, Nobby Stiles scores the only goal of the game. Alan Ball looks on.

5. July 1966 and England take on Portugal in the semi-final. The two airborne players helped to make the game a masterpiece of football. Eusébio (left) and Nobby Stiles (right).

6. The Gerry Byrne final. Liverpool victors at Wembley in May 1965. Gerry Byrne holding the lid of the FA Cup aloft (back right) with his left hand as his right arm hangs limply by his side. Kneeling at the front, far right, is Ian Callaghan and on his right is Roger Hunt.

7. Mrs Cissie Charlton arrives at King's Cross almost to a hero's welcome. She had two sons in the final, Bobby and Jack.

8. World Cup Willie, the first of many World Cup Mascots. Leo Hoye, son of his creator Reg Hoye, supports his press call.

Next spread: 9. Her Majesty the Queen presents Bobby Moore with the Jules Remit Trophy as captain of England. Behind him are Bobby Charlton, Geoff Hurst and Roger Hunt.

10. Home of English soccer. Wembley Stadium was the venue for all of England's games in the 1966 World Cup finals. The redevelopment didn't forget the past as Bobby Moore's statue took its place.

11. Behind every successful man … Mr and Mrs Alf Ramsey.

12. Kenneth Wolstenholme, a national treasure.

13. Hugh Johns, unsung hero. I'd love to know what the game was!

14. The great Uwe Seeler (left) of West Germany who could beat six-foot defenders in the air, and Bobby Moore who could beat six-footed attackers on the ground! Exchanging banners before the final.

15. The full squad except Alf Ramsey. Les Cocker standing back row far left; Harold Shepherdson on the far right.

16. The full squad with Alf Ramsey standing far right at the rear.

17. England at Ninian Park, Cardiff, October 1961. Finding pictures of squad members who were not players in the finals and in England shirts isn't easy. Here is Jimmy Armfield (standing far left), Ron Flowers (standing second from right), John Connelly is seated far left. Ron Springett gets into a lot of pics! Standing next to Jimmy Armfield is Bobby Robson. The match ended one-each.

18. Argentina attack in the quarter-finals and airborne Jack Charlton helps Gordon Banks keep yet another clean sheet.

19. May 1966 and England prepare to take on Yugoslavia in a friendly at Wembley. England won two-nil. Jack Charlton is bending forward to tie his bootlaces, and Jimmy Greaves is in the corner. Next to Jack on his far side is Norman Hunter and next to him, this side of Jimmy, is Terry Paine.

20. July 1966, England take on Denmark in Copenhagen and win by two goals to nil. Standing third from left is Peter Bonetti and third from left in the front row is George Eastham who scored one of England's goals. I was unable to find the reason for black armbands.

he'd had a bonfire which had reignited and when he tried to extinguish it, Alan had a heart attack. He died in the early hours of 25 April 2007.

He'd become well-known for wearing a grey flat cap in later years and this was placed on his coffin for the funeral service held in Winchester Cathedral on 3 May. Nobby Stiles reminded the congregation of Alan's travels in the 1966 World Cup final, 'He covered every blade of grass.'

8

Jimmy Greaves: Striker

James Peter Greaves was born on 20 February 1940 in Manor Park, East Ham, London, and is just as famous for his catchphrase 'It's a funny old game' as he is for scoring goal, after goal, after goal in a playing career that spanned twenty-odd years.

Jimmy is England's third-highest international goal scorer, and set another record at Chelsea by scoring forty-one club goals for them in a single season in 1960/61; he is also the highest goal scorer in the history of Tottenham Hotspur and is the highest goal scorer in the history of English top flight football. In fact, he scored on his debut for every club he played for.

He started as he meant to carry on: signing youth forms in 1956, he proceeded to score 114 goals the following season for the Chelsea Youth Team. It wasn't long before the first team beckoned and he ran out for the local derby at Tottenham Hotspur's White Hart Lane on 24 August 1957, in front of 52,580 folk. And scored.

Ever present at Chelsea from 1957 to 1961, he made 157 appearances and scored 124 goals. Not surprisingly he was top league goal scorer in 1959 and again in 1961. At Chelsea he scored five goals in one single game, and on four occasions scored four goals in a game; he also netted thirteen hat-tricks. He was (and still is) the youngest player to score 100 goals in top-class football. Then Chelsea sold him! Jimmy didn't want to leave, and as a mark he scored all four goals against Nottingham Forest at Stamford Bridge on 29 April 1961 – his last game for them. They made him captain for the day.

He went to A. C. Milan and 'hated every minute of it'. What's sad is that he'd turned down a huge offer from Newcastle United. Jimmy was soon back, and he joined the team he'd scored against on his debut: Tottenham Hotspur. The transfer fee was £99,999, which Tottenham Manager Bill Nicholson said was to take any pressure off that might come about for Jimmy if he had had a £100,000 price tag. But latterly Jimmy has said it was Bill Nicholson who didn't want to be the first manager to break through the £100,000 barrier.

However, Jimmy stayed at Tottenham for nine years, from 1961 to 1970, and scored a huge net-full of 266 goals in 379 games: he was the league's top goal scorer for four of those seasons. He won an FA Cup winners' medal in 1962 and again in 1967 – and scored in one of those matches too. Tottenham won the European Cup Winners' Cup in May 1963, and Jimmy scored twice in the five-one defeat of Atlético Madrid. Tottenham Hotspur, therefore, became the first English club to win a European trophy – Atlético Madrid were the holders.

But by 1970 he was beginning to slow down a bit and his future at Tottenham was under question. So West Ham signed him in a deal which took Martin Peters to White Hart Lane in part-exchange – Martin was then rated as the country's most expensive player.

And, naturally, on his debut for West Ham United Jimmy scored – two goals. West Ham went to Maine Road where Manchester City were not having a good day – the final result was Manchester City one, West Ham United five. Come the following January he was led astray, and went boozing in a night club with a few team mates. One of them was Bobby Moore, and West Ham went down by four goals to nil the following day at Blackpool: they heard some well-chosen words from manager Ron Greenwood.

Jimmy decided to retire, and at the end of the 1970/71 season he hung up his boots – his last competitive game was when Huddersfield Town came down to Upton Park and took both points. He'd struggled a bit with fitness: he scored thirteen goals in forty games for West Ham, which is a bit of a fall-off in his performance, but looking at things overall, in his 516 games he scored 357 goals, which is a record I hope stays, as he was a real icon.

But his retirement was far too early, and in December 1971 he pulled on his boots again, donned a Brentwood shirt and took to the field. He was thirty-five now, but he did well and was offered a place at Chelmsford City for the 1976/77 season. The following season he was with Barnet and in November 1977 made an appearance in the FA Cup for the first time in six years; he'd taken up a role in midfield but still found his old sparkle, scoring twenty-five goals and taking the accolade of Player of the Season for Barnet. In spring of 1979 he had a brief spell with Woodford Town before finally calling it a day.

In 1980, his book *This One's on Me* showed the world that Jim had difficulties with alcohol – he beat these difficulties to become a role model for anyone else who suffered as he and those around him did.

And in his international debut Jimmy hit the net, even if the side went down four-one. That was on 17 May 1959. He played nearly half the games for England that Bobby Charlton played, even though he scored fewer goals, but it was his amazing strike rate that stands out: he is third in the England goal-scorer stakes behind Bobby Charlton and Gary Lineker. However, Jimmy holds the record for hat-tricks – six in all. He once scored seven goals in three games for England, and in the 1960/61 season topped the all-time per season record when he scored thirteen international goals.

On to 1966 and Jimmy was to be the first-choice striker, but in the group match against France he sustained an injury to his leg which put him out. Geoff Hurst came into the team and scored the winner against Argentina, and in the semi-final against Portugal he won the ball to lay on a goal for Bobby Charlton: Geoff therefore retained his place in the final, where he scored his famous hat-trick. Jimmy was later to comment that he didn't ever feel he had a divine right to play in any game. But his display after England had won may have been badly misunderstood, and his reaction at the time of England's success became well-documented; he was to go on holiday with his wife while the rest of the squad attended an official banquet.

Sadly after the 1966 finals he was to win a mere three more caps and only scored one goal; his final international was against Austria for the one-nil win (not a Jimmy Greaves goal) on 27 May 1967.

In all he played 585 top-level games and scored 410 goals.

However, he did appear in a World Cup competition in 1970, when he entered the World Cup Rally driving a Ford Escort and made it into sixth place. His co-driver was Tony Fall and the trip was from London to Mexico City; they travelled 16,000 miles in thirty-eight days – through Europe and South America (Portugal to Brazil). Tony was a veteran rally driver with vast experience.

I mentioned Jimmy's alcoholism earlier, and it's recorded that he hasn't taken a drop for over thirty-five years. This is a big achievement, and people have commented (less so as the years have gone past) that Jimmy was a role model. When he became dry he was able to embark on a very successful television broadcasting career, teaming up with Ian St John to create *Saint and Greavsie*, which ran for seven years. He was often on TV-am discussing football and was featured in the quiz programme *Sporting Triangles*, as well as doing a kids' show on Saturdays.

When Jim was ill once, his place was taken by a *Spitting Image* puppet.

He was also good with the pen, writing regularly for *The Sun* newspaper and replying to readers' letters in *Shoot* magazine. He teamed up with Norman Giller and produced a considerable number of books, and he now does a bit of after-dinner speaking.

Jimmy has medals for winning the FA Cup twice, the Charity Shield twice, and he won the European Cup Winners' Cup. He received his belated World Cup winner's medal in 2009.

He married Irene Barden in March 1958 and they had four children: Lynn, Mitzi, Daniel and Andrew. Daniel played for Southend United and Cambridge United, and went into football management.

9

Bobby Charlton – Midfield: Attack

Sir Robert 'Bobby' Charlton was born in Ashington in Northumberland on 11 October 1937, and is rightly regarded as one of the greatest footballers of all time. He was an essential member of the England team in 1966, and also Manchester United, where he spent the bulk of his playing career.

In 1966 he won the Ballon d'Or, also won by team mates Denis Law and George Best. Cristiano Ronaldo won the accolade in 2008, and it went to another resident of Lancashire when Sir Stanley Matthews won it in its inaugural year of 1956. It is loosely known as the European Footballer of the Year award.

Bobby had very good attacking instincts in the game and his shooting was ferocious; he scored some cracking goals with long-range shots, though did say once that one goalkeeper he'd never shoot at from outside the eighteen-yard box was Gordon Banks, because he felt Gordon always managed to get them.

He made his debut for the first team at Manchester United in 1956 – the era of the Busby Babes. He gained a regular place in the team and in 1958 was rescued by Harry Gregg from the wreckage at the Munich air crash. He has lifted the World Cup, European Cup, League Championship, FA Cup, and Charity Shield. He scored two goals in the European Cup final as captain, and has scored more goals for Manchester United, and England too for that matter, than any other player. Bobby held the record for the most appearances for Manchester United, before being passed by Ryan Giggs.

After a glittering career he left Manchester United to become manager of Preston North End for the 1973/74 season, but then was player/manager the following season. For a brief period in 1983 he was manager of the then Third Division Wigan Athletic; the final match of the 1982/83 season was when Wigan lost at home to Bobby's former club Preston North End. In 1984 he joined Manchester United's board of directors.

Football is in his blood – his brother Jack is well documented here. For uncles he had Jack Milburn of Leeds United and Bradford City, George Milburn of Leeds United and Chesterfield, Jim Milburn of Leeds United and Bradford City, Stan Milburn of Chesterfield, Leicester City and Rochdale, and the legendary Jackie Milburn of Newcastle United and England. With such a distinguished host of mentors its surprising Bobby describes his grandfather Tanner (John Thomas Milburn) and his mother Cissie (Elizabeth Ellen Charlton) as his major early influences.

In his 2009 book, *My Life in Football*, Bobby quotes Jack – 'Everybody in Ashington knew he was special. They all said he would play for England, and he did.'

Joe Armstrong, who was Chief Scout for Manchester United, saw Bobby playing for East Northumberland schools, and he went on to play for England Schoolboys. Bobby signed for Manchester as a fifteen-year-old on 1 January 1953. He wasn't alone, as another fifteen-year-old signed the exact same day; his name was Wilf McGuinness.

He had started an apprenticeship as an electrical engineer, as his mother was a bit nervous of the uncertain world of the professional footballer – and with her family ties Mrs Charlton would have been well in the know. However, Bobby turned fully professional in October 1954. This was as a part of the rebuilding job Matt Busby was doing after the war. The young group of players were to be known as the Busby Babes. And Bobby didn't disappoint, scoring his way up the ranks from the youth team to the reserve teams, and on 6 October 1956 at Old Trafford he made a scoring (twice) debut for the first team against Charlton Athletic: Manchester United won four-two. What got in the way a bit was his National Service, but being posted at Nesscliffe near Shrewsbury with the Royal Army Ordnance Corps certainly helped. Matt Busby advised him to ask for that posting, and he was in good company because Duncan Edwards was there too.

Bobby's total was twelve goals for his first season of 1954/55, but that was only from fourteen starts; in the return match with Charlton Athletic at The Valley he scored a hat-trick in the five-one win.

They won the League Championship that year, but failed quite alarmingly to win the FA Cup too. In the final they were beaten, but the scoreline of two-one doesn't give away the fact that Aston Villa dominated. Quite early on there was a clash between the Manchester United goalkeeper Ray Wood and Aston Villa striker Peter McParland – it was nobody's fault, but Ray sustained a broken cheekbone and had to go off – and as there were no substitutes in those days, Jackie Blanchflower took over in goal. Peter McParland netted the goals twice for Aston Villa and Tommy Taylor for Manchester United.

Bobby had well and truly established himself, and as league champions the team were entered for the European Cup: the first English club to compete. Manchester United did well, and progressed as far as the semi-finals, where they were defeated by the cup holders, Real Madrid.

The following season they reached European heights again when in the quarter-finals they were drawn against the Yugoslavian champions Red Star Belgrade. Manchester United took a slender lead of two-one into the second leg. In the second game they took a three-nil lead before Red Star mounted a comeback, but still only managed to level the scores at three goals each. But that put the Lancashire club into the semi-finals by an aggregate score of five goals to four. Could they win it this year? Matt Busby wasn't one to rest on his laurels, and they had a league game with Wolverhampton Wanderers at Molineux the following weekend – in fact this match was to be rearranged for 21 April. However, they left Belgrade a happy bunch.

It was a long trip home and the aeroplane needed to refuel, so it landed at Munich amid wintery weather. Soon all was done, and they were ready for the final leg of the journey. Snow had fallen; the plane accelerated down the runway but the captain had to abort the take-off as they couldn't attain the speed. The aeroplane was checked over by mechanics and a second take-off run showed up the same problem. The passengers returned to the terminal and nerves were getting a little frayed. The snow had continued to fall. On the third take-off run the right speed was just about attained, and the aeroplane was just set to become airborne when it hit a patch of ice and slush – not a huge issue, but the captain was committed to taking off, and the ice and slush had just taken the edge off the power. The aeroplane left the ground but clipped the fence at the end of the runway and couldn't climb quickly enough to avoid the house into which it then crashed.

Bobby survived, rescued by Harry Gregg the goalkeeper – Harry rescued more folk too. But twenty-three people died, eight of whom were in Manchester United's first team. And of the eight players who did survive, two were too badly injured to recover and play again. According to the German investigators, the crash was caused by pilot error, but that has largely been disproved. The cause was the weather conditions – try driving a car through a large puddle and the edge will be taken off the power. Captain James Thain was exonerated on this side of the Channel, but the German air crash investigator was unwilling to listen to any arguments, despite much evidence. It was actually the co-pilot, Kenneth Raiment, who had been flying the aeroplane, and he had actually been sat in the captain's seat – this became an issue. But both Captain Thain and Captain Raiment were vastly experienced pilots.

Bobby returned to the pitch on 1 March in an FA Cup match against West Bromwich Albion which finished in a draw, but Manchester United won the replay by a goal to nil. With such a loss of skill and a feeling of mourning for those departed, their league performance suffered. They were knocked out of the European Cup by AC Milan in a five-two aggregate score.

Matt Busby was laid up for a while, but was able to oversee the FA Cup final in which they were to meet Bolton Wanderers. Nat Lofthouse scored twice to take the cup back to Burnden Park.

The team recovered, but even in the early 1970s when Bobby was a guest on *This Is Your Life* the pain and trauma were still evident.

The rebuilding of the club was to take a number of years, but in 1963 Bobby was on the winning side in the FA Cup final, as Manchester United, who'd struggled a bit with results during the season, took on the high-flying Leicester City. The trophy was destined for Old Trafford, the final score three goals to one.

The club then won two League Championships in the mid-1960s – in 1964/65 and again in 1966/67. Bobby Charlton was going from strength to strength and was voted the Football Writers' Footballer of the Year and also the European Footballer of the Year.

In 1968 the most exciting forward line in English club football had established itself with Bobby Charlton, Denis Law and George Best. Their time had come to win the European Cup final, but they were up against Eusébio's Benfica, so a night of huge entertainment got under way. At the end of ninety minutes on the gruelling Wembley pitch the sides were all square on a goal each. But Bobby, as captain, was to lift the trophy, because with three goals scored in extra time (Bob scored two in the whole game) they'd done it – not only were they the first English club to make the final, but the first to win – and winning in such style was a terrific accomplishment.

But after every peak a trough is possible, and Manchester United's was quite a deep one. There were tensions, too, in the relationships of the three men up front. Bobby left Manchester United at the end of the 1972/73 season: he'd made 758 appearances and scored 249 goals. It would take a player of equal calibre to break this record: Ryan Giggs did so, much to Bobby's delight – it meant Manchester United, where his heart was, was a great force again. But Sir Bobby's goal-scoring record is still to be beaten. His final goal in a Manchester United shirt came on 31 March 1973 at Southampton; his final appearance was at Stamford Bridge, when Chelsea beat Manchester United by a goal to nil.

Just over two months after the Munich crash, Bobby was called up to play for England. On 19 April 1958 Walter Winterbottom's men took on the Scots at Hampden Park and beat them by four goals to nil – Tom Finney crossed for Bobby to send a 'thumping volley' into the net. Then Bobby scored both goals as he made his Wembley entrance, England beating Portugal by two goals to one. After that came a sad return to Belgrade, where England were well and truly demolished with five goals to nil. It might not have been a pleasant experience for Bobby, but at least he was overcoming the clear knock Munich had given him.

In the 1958 World Cup finals in Sweden he was in the squad, but didn't actually play, which brought on surprise and criticism – surely he had been entitled to lose concentration that day in Belgrade? But there was a selection committee in those days, so one wonders.

Not one to be put down, Bob started to score hat-tricks – first in 1959 as England demolished America and then two years later against Mexico as England cruised to an eight-nil win. In the Home Internationals he was usually on the score sheet.

He was twenty-four when the qualifying matches for the 1962 World Cup finals were played, and Luxemburg and Portugal were dispatched. In Chile that year Bobby scored in the three-one group win over Argentina – on his thirty- eighth appearance he scored his twenty-fifth international goal. England went through to the quarter-finals, where they were beaten by Brazil.

Shortly after, Alf Ramsey, landed the England manager's

job and straight away announced that England would win the next World Cup, which was to be held in London. Alf had quite bluntly told the FA that the selection committee for the side was unacceptable as he started the job of building the Team of 66. And Alf was the boss – he expected loyalty, but also ability and form, and above all he expected good behaviour on the pitch. Bobby never let him down, although there was some talk of him being cautioned in the match with Argentina in the 1966 quarter-finals, but the referee that day really had his work cut out.

The goals kept coming: another hat-trick in an eight-one defeat of Switzerland in mid-1963 took his goal record to thirty, thus equalling the joint record of Nat Lofthouse and Tom Finney, and in October 1963 when he scored against Wales at Ninian Park, he took the record.

Alf was leading a dynamic side in a developing game – the formations of the teams were changing, and two wingers and two inside forwards were being phased out. Bobby had developed away from the inside forward type of role to what would be an attacking midfielder. In May 1964 Bobby scored his thirty-third goal for his country. In his new role the goals would dwindle a bit, but his role was to create chances as well as to score them. When the finals of the World Cup were approaching in 1966, the whole world knew that with Bobby Charlton they were to see someone special.

After a dull opening match with Uruguay, the side took to the field against Mexico. Bobby's next goal was a question of when and not if. The opening goal was a pure piece of magic, and later a second goal sealed the victory. Another two-nil win against the French made sure of England's progression to the quarter-finals, where a hard-playing Argentina made them work hard for their win, even though the Argentinians were down to ten men from only about half way through the first half.

In the semi-finals England took on Portugal for one of the best games of football ever played. Roger Hunt made a run which took the goalkeeper to the side of the goal, and when the ball found Bobby, a neat side-foot shot into the goal ensued. In the second half Geoff Hurst led an attack which took him into the eighteen-yard box with Bobby in support – a neat lay-back and Bobby scored England's second goal. So good was it that even the Portuguese players applauded and congratulated him.

Then came the clash with West Germany in the final. For Bobby this was a quiet day as he and Franz Beckenbauer marked each other out of the game.

So England were World Champions, and their sights were now firmly set on the European Championships; in Belfast in October 1966 England had a two-nil victory. Just about three weeks later Bobby scored again for his country in a convincing win over Wales at Wembley.

Jimmy Greaves had become the leading English marksman in 1967, but in a friendly against Sweden Bobby took the crown from him with his forty-fifth goal.

England were defeated by Yugoslavia, so met the Russians in the third-place play-off in the European Championships. Bob scored, but after that there followed a bit of a famine, which lasted until 7 May 1969. Bob was awarded an OBE in 1969 for his services to football.

There was a rather uneventful tour of Latin America in the summer of that year which saw his position in central to attacking midfield become even more valuable to the national team, as the appearance of wingers continued to decline.

On 21 April 1970 Bobby, as captain, led England out against Northern Ireland at Wembley. Martin Peters converted a corner from Bobby, and later he started a move that saw Geoff Hurst get on the score sheet, before Bobby side-footed in the third goal ten minutes from time – that was the evening of his 100th cap for England, and by then only one other player in history had attained over the 100 mark, that being Billy Wright. He had now scored forty-eight goals. His forty-ninth would come many miles away from England in a four-nil win against Columbia in the warm-up tour for the 1970 World Cup finals.

The 1970 World Cup finals in Mexico was to be Bobby's fourth tournament, but in the pre-tournament tour in Bogotà the notorious bracelet incident occurred, and although Bobby Charlton wasn't arrested, Bobby Moore was, and the whole team mechanics Alf Ramsey had created came under threat.

'Back Home they'll be thinkin' about us', etc. – these are lines from a hit record by the 1970 squad. The television coverage was as good for that tournament as it had been for the 1966 finals, and all was now in colour. The BBC put together a package of seventy hours of coverage.

England's opening game in defence of their world title

came against a physically robust Romanian side, which made for dour viewing. The one incident to excite came in the sixty-fifth minute, when Alan Ball and Francis Lee combined to send the ball forward to Geoff Hurst, who then scored the only goal of the game. Brazil had beaten Czechoslovakia by a robust four goals to one, but the England win against the Romanians upset the locals, who caused a bit of a noise – most nights and all night – outside England's hotel.

On Sunday 7 June 1970 the match of the tournament took place as Brazil and England – past champions, current champions and future champions – came face to face. The game was a magnificent display of skill and, as usual with the Brazilians, excitement was created from nothing. Alf Ramsey was confident of qualifying for the last sixteen, so substituted Bobby with Colin Bell. He did the same against Czechoslovakia four days later when Alan Ball came on. Bobby was now thirty-two, so Alf wanted him to rest, and playing in that heat in Mexico the players lost a couple of pounds per match.

In the quarter-finals Bobby came up against Franz Beckenbauer again, but things had moved on in the four years since the Wembley show-down. In fact, Bobby controlled the midfield and gave Franz very little leeway, and both Alan Mullery and Martin Peters' goals – both created by the full back/winger Keith Newton – made England comfortable. But when Franz got away from Bobby and was able to make one of his deep runs, his final shot went under Peter Bonetti's body and pulled a goal back. Gordon Banks had been sidelined with a tummy bug, which had been a bit of a blow, but no matter. Just after the West German goal, Bobby went off and Colin Bell came on as substitute.

The last twenty minutes saw the West Germans effectively take control and a superb header from the portly Uwe Seeler secured the equaliser, though England did have a couple of chances to redeem themselves. But the West Germans scored in extra time and that was the end of England's reign as World Champions. The story has now developed and reports that it was after Bobby left the field that the tide turned and the West Germans started looking more likely winners, but this is not borne out by the facts: Franz Beckenbauer scored before Bob was substituted, so that made little difference and Colin Bell was Bob's equal.

That was when he set the record of 106 caps for his country, and on the plane home he explained to Alf that he didn't feel he could do the cause any more good. His forty-nine international goals remain a record. His cap tally was passed three years later when Bobby Moore made his 107th appearance, and later Peter Shilton and then David Beckham would pass it too.

In May 1973 Bobby was appointed manager of Preston North End, and took the aspiring player/coach Nobby Stiles away from Middlesbrough as his second in command. His first season didn't go too well and the club were relegated to the Third Division. The following season he started playing again, but his management record would not be too hot. He left Preston in the autumn of 1975 because he was not happy about the transfer of a player to Newcastle United.

Bobby went to the Republic of Ireland and played three matches for Waterford United, scoring one goal. Bobby then started a long association with the BBC as football pundit.

He went to Wigan Athletic as a director, and was briefly caretaker manager there in 1983. He then spent a short time playing in South Africa. He also built up several businesses in areas such as travel, jewellery and hampers, and ran soccer schools in the UK, the US, Canada, Australia and China. In 1984, he was invited to become a member of the board of directors at Manchester United, partly because of his football knowledge and partly because it was felt that the club needed a 'name' on the board after the retirement of Sir Matt Busby.

In 1961 he had met Norma Ball at an ice rink, and they married a couple of years later. They had two daughters, Suzanne and Andrea. Suzanne became a weather forecaster with the BBC for a good while. Bobby and Norma now have grandchildren.

Like most other families, the Charltons have had their falling outs. Sometimes the in-law relationship is not one made in heaven, and sadly Norma and Cissie Charlton didn't always see eye-to-eye. In such situations it is almost impossible to remain neutral, and Bobby and his mother didn't see too much of each other – she died aged eighty-three in 1996. This led to a long stand-off between Bobby and Jack. But the BBC did help the bridge-building by asking Jack to present Bobby with the BBC Sports Personality Lifetime Achievement in December 2008.

There was a standing ovation as he stood waiting for his prize. Going back to 1966, one of the best sights in the finals tournament was Jack congratulating Bob for scoring a goal.

Bobby and Norma Charlton became Sir Bobby and Lady Norma in 1994, and Bob worked tirelessly for Manchester's bids for the Olympic and Commonwealth games, as well the bid for the World Cup and the 2012 Olympics.

Sir Bobby was an inaugural inductee to the English Football Hall of Fame in 2002. On accepting the accolade he said, 'I'm really proud to be included in the National Football Museum's Hall of Fame. It's a great honour. If you look at the names included I have to say I couldn't argue with them. They are all great players and people I would love to have played with.'

He's also the president of the National Football Museum, an organisation about which he said, 'I can't think of a better Museum anywhere in the world.'

On 2 March 2009, Sir Bobby was given the freedom of the city of Manchester, stating, 'I'm just so proud, it's fantastic. It's a great city. I have always been very proud of it.'

He has a number of interests in charities, which, similar to many players of the 1966 squad, include the various cancer charities. He has also taken an interest in the land-mine issues and founded the charity *Find A Better Way*, which is engaged in land-mine clearance.

So where would the Manchester United supporters put him in the list of all-time greats? That might be academic, as one poll put him behind Ryan Giggs, Eric Canton and George Best. There is no denying those players deserve the accolade, but there might be others from the pre-television era or going back a few generations that could be included: choosing the great players from 'all-time' leaves a lot of doors open.

10

Geoff Hurst – Striker

Sir Geoffrey Charles, or 'Geoff', Hurst was born on 8 December 1941 in Ashton-Under-Lyne in Lancashire and he was, and remains, the only player to score a hat-trick in a World Cup final.

He was a striker of some consistency too, as he scored a total of 242 goals in 500 games for West Ham United. With Geoff, West Ham won the FA Cup in 1964 and the European Cup Winners' Cup the following season. His strike rate for England was almost identical; he scored twenty-four goals in forty-nine games.

Although he was born in Lancashire, his family moved to Chelmsford in Essex when he was six. His father had been a footballer (a centre half), and had played for Bristol Rovers before serving two clubs in Lancashire: Oldham Athletic and Rochdale. Bristol was in Gloucestershire in those days and Geoff's mother, Evelyn, was from Gloucestershire, though her roots have been traced to the Continent.

Sons of professional footballers can go one way or another, and Geoff was an all-round sportsman with a love of cricket. He was a good wicketkeeper for the Essex Second Eleven in the early 1960s, but football was to get his full attention. His enthusiasm for football got him into a bit of trouble as he was growing up, and there was talk of a fine for disturbing the peace.

By the time he geared down his willow activities he was well past his apprenticeship in football with West Ham United, which he started in 1956 under the overall management of Ted Fenton. Geoff made a relatively senior appearance for the first time in the Southern Floodlit Cup against Fulham at the end of 1958. He turned professional in the spring of 1959 and was given a £20 signing on fee; his wages were to be £7 a week.

Injuries piled up at West Ham, so Geoff made his first senior appearance at The City Ground of Nottingham Forest in February 1962. He failed to impress at left half, which was another junior player's favoured position – one Bobby Moore. Geoff only made a total of three appearances in the 1959/60 season and was selected only six times in the following season. He started to hanker after cricket again, but then Ted Fenton and the club parted company and Ron Greenwood took over. Ron wanted the players to focus on the finer points of footballing skills, with fitness coming a close second in his list of priorities. This would prove the deciding point in Geoff's choice of career.

In the 1961/62 season Geoff made twenty-four appearances at left half and on 18 December 1961 at Upton Park he scored his first goal when West Ham beat Wolverhampton Wanderers by four goals to two. But Ron Greenwood questioned whether he was best suited to a defensive role, and thought he'd try him up front. In the 1962/63 season, in partnership with Johnny Byrne, Geoff found the net thirteen times from twenty-seven starts in the First Division.

In the summer of 1963 West Ham took part in a friendly tournament with other clubs from other parts of the world in New York. But back home for the 1963/64 season West Ham didn't fare too well, and finished mid-table at the end of the season.

However, their FA Cup run that year saw them lift the trophy for the first time in their history. In the third round they defeated Charlton Athletic by three goals to nil at home, and then another London team were dispatched with a three-nil defeat; that team being Leyton Orient. They had to work a bit for this victory as it had gone to a replay – the teams drew a goal apiece at Brisbane Road initially. West Ham then went to Swindon, where they won by three goals to one. At Upton Park, the sixth round saw them beat Burnley three-two. Goals kept coming Geoff's way. In the semi-finals they met Manchester United at Hillsborough, and a move initiated by Bobby Moore would see Geoff get the third and decisive goal in a three-one win. In the final they were to take on Preston North End, who then were a Second Division outfit, and twice West Ham had to equalise before they could get their third and match-winning goal. Geoff scored the second equaliser. One lucky break for Ron Greenwood was that he could field an unchanged side in each round.

This meant European football in the European Cup Winners' Cup the following season. KAA Gent of Belgium gave them an unconvincing two-one aggregate victory, and Sparta Prague went down by the odd goal in five in the next round. The Swiss FC Lausanne-Sport went down by six goals to four, and Geoff was still to score in the competition, so Ron suggested he drop behind John Byrne and take more of an attacking midfield role. In the semi-finals they just squeezed a two-one win against the Spanish club Real Zaragoza, but held them to a draw in Spain. They'd made the final, and they were to meet the German club TSV 1860 München. The final was played at Wembley Stadium, and Alan Sealy scored the goals that gave West Ham their first European trophy.

West Ham United could have added the Football League Cup to their cabinet, but went down by five goals to three against West Bromwich Albion.

Geoff's league form was hotting up, and he scored forty goals in fifty-nine games in the 1965/66 season. His performance, which I'll discuss shortly, in the 1966 World Cup finals, prompted Matt Busby to offer £200,000 for his services, and Ron Greenwood was prompted to say 'No'. The record transfer at that time was £115,000, which had taken Denis Law back to the UK and Manchester United. £200,000 would have been a massive leap – in fact it wasn't until four years or so later, when Martin Peters left

West Ham United for Tottenham Hotspur, that the figure was equalled.

He was devoted to attacking football and, very much like Ron Greenwood, wouldn't give that up to win trophies. But West Ham was inconsistent; in the 1966/67 season they demolished first-division big boys Leeds United in the League Cup, but then went down three-one in the FA Cup to third-division Swindon Town.

Geoff's career wasn't marked by controversy, but he learned not to talk to the press if he could help it. On 19 October 1968 West Ham beat Sunderland eight-nil. Geoff scored six of these, so the press were eager for something or other. Geoff admitted handling the ball, so the headlines on the sports pages made a big issue of this and not his final tally.

Geoff would often be penalty taker for West Ham, but if the goalkeeper remembered the tactics he tended to use then Geoff might be in trouble: he took a penalty for West Ham against Stoke City, but Stoke goalkeeper Gordon Banks remembered. In the semi-finals of the Football League Cup in 1972 Harry Rednapp was pulled down in the eighteen-yard box. Up steamed Geoff, and walloped the ball high towards the top corner – exactly where Gordon had predicted he would. He got a hand to it and the ball went over the bar. In Gordon's *This Is Your Life* a few months later, the host Eamonn Andrews reminded Geoff, and he wasn't too enchanted.

On the subject of Stoke City, Tony Waddington, their manager, offered West Ham £80,000 for Geoff in August 1972, so off he went to The Potteries. He contracted pneumonia a few months later, and played on loan to Cape Town City in sunnier climes to complete his recovery.

Stoke City were often just above the relegation zone, but they were buoyant with Geoff on board, and as he only missed four games in the 1972/73 season, Stoke finished in fifteenth position in the First Division.

Tony Waddington used Geoff's stable home life to try and steady new signing from Chelsea, Alan Hudson. It was a success, but I gather quite a lot went on on Tony Waddington's 'blind side'. Together, the two players lifted Stoke City to fifth place in the league in 1973/74, which was as high as Geoff was to get!

In his final season at Stoke City, 1974/75, he scored eleven goals in forty-one games. West Bromwich Albion manager, Johnny Giles, then paid £20,000 for him. He played twelve games at The Hawthorns and scored twice before leaving the club – at the age of thirty-four he felt his best days were behind him.

Geoff signed for Cork Celtic in January 1976, and stayed a month. Then he signed for the Seattle Sounders of the North American Soccer League (NASL) later that year. He soon proved his worth, and became a valuable member of the Sounders team, being the second-highest scorer and helping the Sounders make it to the knock-out play-offs for the first time in their history. He scored eight goals in twenty-three games, and one goal in the play-offs.

At the time of the 1966 World Cup finals, Geoff had only made four appearances for England and had only made his debut the February before in a one-nil win against West Germany at Wembley.

He had also played in games against Scotland and Yugoslavia, and his performance secured his place in the twenty-two man squad. In a short pre-tournament tour of Europe Geoff didn't do particularly well; Jimmy Greaves and Roger Hunt had gelled together for the final game of the tour against Poland so Alf had chosen those two to lead the attack once the tournament started. They produced no magical goal spree against Uruguay, but picked up a bit against Mexico, with Roger netting one goal and Bobby Charlton the other. The strike force came into its own against France with a brace of goals for Roger, but Jimmy sustained a large gash in his leg which ruled him out of the quarter-finals.

Argentina really let England off the hook; in the quarter-finals they didn't display the skills they could have, which would really have made for a spectacle. Instead there was some suggestion of off-the-ball physical stuff on the blind side of the referee. The referee didn't get quite the hold on the game one would have liked, and eventually Argentina were down to ten men. But when the match did settle down it was worthwhile, and again the West Ham link-up was to prove fruitful. With about fifteen minutes left on the clock Martin Peters came down the left flank and could see Geoff lurking in the centre – he sent a curling cross to the near-post and Geoff, away from his marker, put in a glancing header to guide the ball into the net. So England reached the semi-finals.

The semi-final came only three days later and Jimmy Greaves still wasn't match fit, so Geoff and Roger continued to spearhead the attack. Bobby Charlton scored twice for England to secure an historic win, but the second goal was a gift from Geoff: he had taken the ball to the byline and skilfully extricated himself to get into a scoring position. However when he looked up he saw the lone figure of Bobby, who, receiving the lay-back, hammered the ball home. Eusébio's penalty late on in the game was the first goal England conceded in the tournament.

Jimmy Greaves had recovered his match fitness and as soon as the press heard about this they were on to Alf to bring him back into the side. Alf, however, wouldn't change a winning side – Geoff would be up front again in the final.

Helmut Haller scored a great goal but had the English defence to thank for it, however six minutes later Geoff connected perfectly to Bobby Moore's free kick, with West German defenders on all sides, to head home the equaliser. About twenty minutes later half time came and went, with the sides having a goal each. The second half got underway but with the grace of Bobby Charlton, the determination of Alan Ball and the tenacity of Nobby Stiles, the midfield was all England. In the seventy-eighth minute Alan Ball took a corner, but it seemed to drift out and away from the goal – Geoff then hit it hard in what looked like an effort for the goal, but Wolfgang Weber got a foot to it and it cannoned off into the air, falling inch perfect at Martin Peters' foot – so England took the lead. The famous goal-mouth scramble a few seconds before the final whistle saw the equaliser.

In the first period of extra time, Alan Ball galloped

down the right flank and made a first-time cross to the near post to Geoff, who was in acres of space courtesy of Roger Hunt running a bit wide. Geoff took the ball and turned to strike a strong shot towards goal with his right foot, falling backwards as he did so. The ball beat the goalkeeper, hit the crossbar and bounced down before it was headed out for what might have been a corner. England's players claimed a goal, while the West Germans were adamant that the ball hadn't crossed the line. Referee Gottfried Dienst came across to the linesman Tofiq Bahramov, who had no doubt, and the goal was given. Controversy has raged ever since.

With nothing to lose, the West Germans pushed forward in number, and as the full-time whistle approached Bobby Moore sent a long ball out of defence and Geoff picked it up in the West German half of the field. When he reached the eighteen-yard box he thought if he just blasted the ball anywhere the final whistle would go before any counter-attack could be made. Fortunately for all concerned – it would have been a shame if the match had been decided on a controversial goal – the ball bounced awkwardly but perfectly, and when Geoff hit it he sent it on a collision course with the back of the net. At four-two, England became World Champions.

That wasn't his only international hat-trick, because in a five-nil win over France on 12 March 1969 he did it again. Geoff lined up for the next game England played in the World Cup, which was against Romania in the group-opener in Mexico in 1970, and he scored the winning goal. That was his last World Cup goal, as England just failed to score against Brazil and Alan Clarke converted the penalty against Czechoslovakia. Alan Mullery and Martin Peters, the latter adequately served by Geoff in the build-up, scored England's two goals in the quarter-final defeat by West Germany.

In the 1972 qualifying games for the European Championships he scored against Greece and then against Switzerland. In England's three-one defeat to West Germany at Wembley he left the pitch twenty minutes from the end and was replaced by Rodney Marsh. So on 29 April 1972 Geoff made his last appearance in an England shirt. He was provisionally in the squad for the return game against West Germany, but pulled out because of injury.

When he finally hung up his boots, Geoff wanted to get a grounding in coaching and management. He was at Telford United as player/manager for three years before he rejoined the international set-up when Ron Greenwood became England Manager in 1977. He was away with the squad for the European Championships in 1980 and was at the World Cup finals in 1982; England didn't even get past the group stage.

He joined Chelsea as assistant to Danny Blanchflower just before the start of the 1979/80 season, and when Danny was sacked he became manager. Bobby Gould came in as his assistant and things looked set to go well. As a second-division side Chelsea wanted to get back into the top flight, and that seemed something they could have achieved, but in their final seven games they only managed two wins and the club missed out on promotion, finishing fourth.

Geoff set about rebuilding the squad, selling three players and buying three, but one of his new players didn't settle and another had some bad luck with a series of injuries.

Things started well in the first part of the 1980/81 season with Chelsea taking points in an eleven-game unbeaten run, but after the winter months the rot set in, including another run of games without a win. In fact Chelsea only scored three goals in over twenty league fixtures. Geoff was sacked at the end of the season.

He then went into the insurance industry. Kuwait SC then offered him a big salary to manage them in their premier league, but it didn't work out too well, and Geoff returned to the insurance industry in 1984.

Close to West Ham's Upton Park is a statue, *The Champions*, in which Geoff, together with Bobby Moore, Martin Peters and Ray Wilson, hold the 1966 trophy. Geoff was knighted in 1998. In 2004 he was inducted to the English Football Hall of fame.

He married Judith Harries on 13 October 1964. They were to have three daughters: Claire in 1965 (sadly she passed away in 2010), Joanne, who was born in 1969, and Charlotte, who came along in 1977. There are now grandchildren. The couple live in Cheltenham, Gloucestershire.

11

John Connelly – Striker: Winger

It was his twentieth international for England, and there were about five minutes left for play. Ray Wilson was out on the far left teeing up a good winger's cross, Jack Charlton was just about on the penalty spot, and was head and shoulders above two Uruguayan defenders as he headed the ball powerfully on to another England head, this time on the shoulders of John Connelly. His header hit the woodwork (he was a joiner by trade), but it looked as though it was off-side – by about half the thickness of the paint on the cross-bar – and so John was the closest to scoring the opening goal in the 1966 World Cup finals in the opening match.

Sadly that was his last match for England. Alf Ramsey wanted his full backs to double up as wingers, and that was John's usual place. The lad from the rugby stronghold of St Helens who had never played a club home game outside of Lancashire was a classic example of the perfect player. His first League Championship medal came for his first club of Burnley, but then he joined mighty Manchester United to complete the forward line with George Best, Bobby Charlton, Denis Law and David Herd – with that lot it wasn't a case of if he were to win a championship medal again, but when!

John was born in 1938 and had a brother, Jimmy, who was about five years younger. He started his working life as an apprenticeship joiner as his father was keen for him to get a trade, but his footballing instincts were to come through. A classic winger but a high goal scorer, out of 527 club games he scored 200 goals, better than one in three, and his ration for England was seven goals in twenty games.

He married Alexandra (Sandra) in 1958; Nicola was born in 1962 and was soon joined by Debra. Jonathan came a couple of years after the 1966 triumph.

He had joined Burnley in 1956 when scouts had gone to watch his team mate play! He had to wait a while to secure a first-team place, but he made his debut in a one-all draw at Leeds United in March 1957. His game was hallmarked by his speed and ability to cross the ball, and he could also mimic an inside forward by cutting inside – no doubt driving more than one full back to distraction. He moved from the right wing to the left wing when a young Willie Morgan joined the side. He had a cartilage operation at the end of the 1959/60 season, and it wasn't until the very last game at Manchester City that Burnley just pipped the Wolverhampton Wanderers to the league trophy.

As the crow flies it is about twenty-four miles from Turf Moor to Old Trafford, and John made the journey to the Matt Busby empire in April 1964: a cheque for £56,000 made the opposite journey.

He'd already made his full England debut at Ninian Park against Wales in October 1959, where a fresh-faced Jimmy Greaves, making his second appearance, scored after thirty minutes. Joining him and John was Brian Clough – Graham Moore equalised for Wales just before time. Earning his second cap against Sweden at the end of the month at Wembley, John scored the opening goal. He won ten of his international caps while with Burnley.

For Manchester United he played for just over two seasons, making 113 appearances and scoring 35 goals. In 1964/65, Manchester United won the league on goal average from Leeds United, with Chelsea a close third. He had two more seasons and ten more international caps before joining Blackburn Rovers for £40,000 in late 1966. Unfortunately Blackburn had just been relegated to the Second Division.

John enjoyed four seasons at Blackburn, who remained in the Second Division. After the 1969/70 season he was released by Blackburn and made the short journey to Bury, where he thrilled for three more seasons before hanging up his boots.

John Connelly was a very modest man, who abandoned an autobiography, thinking he'd been forgotten. He had toyed with the idea of *John Who* for a title. But he wore the number seven shirt for Manchester United – so did David Beckham, Eric Cantona and Bryan Robson. It's unlikely he will ever be forgotten.

Something else he was proud of, and that is the very English is fish and chips; he ran Connelly's Plaice in Brierfield (still there I think) for over thirty years with his wife. The taste was legendary. He also liked a pint of beer (Bass), and when he was awarded his belated medal for 1966 he took it to his local to show it off – not quite in keeping with his modesty, but who would begrudge him the pride.

John also served his community as a Justice of the Peace.

On 25 October 2012 he lost his battle with bone cancer and passed away at his home. Burnley made the announcement, 'One of Burnley's most prolific and popular wingers, he died peacefully at home on Thursday morning.' He was seventy-four.

12

Ron Springett – Goalkeeper.

Ron Springett was to make 33 appearances for the England national side, but none in the 1966 finals. He was born in Fulham in London in July 1935. His younger brother, Peter, was also a professional footballer, and a goalkeeper. Ron started on the road to glory under Alec Stock at Queens Park Rangers (QPR). His local club Fulham had turned him down. He married Barbara in 1958 and that same year was transferred to Sheffield Wednesday for £10,000. He was to make 384 appearances for the Hillsborough side before returning to QPR in 1967 in a unique transfer that took his brother to Sheffield Wednesday. While at QPR Ron played in ninety-eight club and league games before he went to Sheffield Wednesday: when he returned he played another forty-nine.

He made his international debut against Northern Ireland at Wembley on 18 November 1959, and Joe Baker put them ahead after sixteen minutes. Billy Bingham must have made Ron's heart sink when he equalised two minutes from time but Bolton Wanderer Ray Parry wrapped up the game at two-one just before time. And Ron saved a Jimmy McIlroy penalty.

Under Walter Winterbottom, Ron made most of his England appearances. He was a great friend of Gordon Banks and there was at least one occasion Gordon mentions in his autobiography where Ron came to his house for lunch before a match against Gordon's side. He was well respected and had modelled his goalkeeping on Manchester City's Bert Trautmann: he found that he could get greater accuracy and start a counter-attack more efficiently by throwing the ball out rather than the big boot upfield.

He had been the goalkeeper of choice in the Chile World Cup finals in 1962. Ron had what was described as a 'nightmare game' against France in Paris in February 1963 and the new England manager, Alf Ramsey, pushed Gordon Banks into the line-up for the next international against Scotland.

Fast forwarding to 1966, the World Cup finals were preceded by a short tour of Europe – in which Martin Peters won his first cap. Both Ron Springett and Peter Bonetti played in goal during this tour, Ron against a Norwegian side in a six goals to one win in Oslo. That was Ron's last England cap.

He and Barbara had two children.

13

Peter Bonetti – Goalkeeper

Peter was twenty-four by the time the 1966 tournament came round and had only been capped for England once. He was born in Putney in London in late September 1941. His parents had hailed from Switzerland. When Peter was young the family moved to Worthing on the South Coast, where he grew up among many siblings and where his parents ran a coffee bar. He married Francis in 1962 and they had four kids – three girls and a boy. After his footballing career he was a postman on the Isle of Mull but made a bit of a comeback with Dundee United before heading for glory in America with the St Louis Stars. These days he lives in Sutton Coldfield with his second wife, Kay.

By the time Peter hung up his gloves he had made seven

appearances for the full England side, following twelve at under-23 level. For his main and only real football club, Chelsea, Peter made 729 appearances in which he kept 208 clean sheets, a record only just passed.

His honours at club level began in 1965 when, over the two-legged Football League Cup final, he played a blinder and Chelsea beat Gordon Banks' Leicester City on aggregate. In 1970 Chelsea reached the final of the FA Cup, where a soft goal from Jack Charlton and a wonderful strike from Mick Jones twice made Chelsea come back, first from (in a disaster for the Leeds goalkeeper Gary Sprake) a soft long-distance strike from Peter Houseman, which slipped under Gary's body. Ian Hutchinson flicked in a perfect header to send both teams to Old Trafford for a replay. Peter was the undisputable hero that night. A clash with Alan Clarke left him hobbling from early on and he was powerless to stop a Mick Jones strike soon after. But Chelsea rallied, with Peter Osgood grabbing the equaliser after a masterful build-up (Jack Charlton said he was kicked), and in extra time David Webb put them ahead.

Most people will remember with sadness Peter Bonetti's last England game when at short notice he stepped into goal against West Germany in the quarter-finals of the 1970 World Cup in Mexico. Gordon Banks was laid up with food poisoning but Peter was world class and based on form England should have won. By mid-second half they were two goals up but then a combination of things – none of which was lack of skill or application – including the searing heat and a little fatigue, saw the spirit of the

West Germans revive, and the luck went with them. Some folk have said Peter might have saved the first goal from Franz Beckenbauer, but that's debateable, and that the match turned when Bobby Charlton went off and Colin Bell came on – the West Germans had already started their fight-back. Imagining for a moment that Gordon was struck down in 1966 and Peter had played in the final, England would have still come out as winners because with Peter's skill, determination and anticipation together with his superb agility, he would have played well. It is unfair to think that if Gordon Banks had been on duty in 1970 the result would have been any different. England were the better side over the ninety minutes, and extra time. Alf Ramsey cursed the luck that had run out for his team, and said of all the players he could have lost it had to be Gordon Banks, but to take this as anything like a criticism of Peter Bonetti is to do poor justice to both Sir Alf and Peter.

Peter and Chelsea were back in the limelight in 1972 when they reached the final of the Football League Cup at Wembley. They made a bad start because lesser-fancied Stoke City took the lead early on through Terry Conroy, but just on the stroke of half time Peter Osgood equalised for Chelsea. Stoke came out in the second half determined not to let the late equaliser upset their momentum, and the veteran George Eastham (he features a little, later on) scored the winner for Stoke City.

For anyone who would still labour the point of Peter's nightmare against West Germany, don't forget there was a defence in front of him. But here are some figures to think about – out of his seven appearances for England he won six, he kept a clean sheet for five of those games, and was only beaten by a single goal on his sixth. 'The three greatest goalkeepers I have ever seen are Gordon Banks, Lev Yashin and Peter Bonetti' (Pele).

By the time Peter was ready to call it a day the value of a goalkeeping coach was becoming realised – and he worked for a time with Chelsea.

14

Jimmy Armfield – Defender: Right Back.

James Christopher Armfield was born in September 1935 and was one of Joe Smith's last finds for Blackpool. He made his debut the day after Boxing Day 1954; not the best of games as they went down three-nil to Portsmouth – and they were a goal down before Jimmy had even made contact with the ball! But he was to become the best right back in the world by the time of the 1962 Chilean World Cup.

So Jimmy joined a team with a number of players of distinction, of which Stanley Matthews is still a household name. But he joined the club a season after the magnificent four-three victory over Bolton Wanderers in the FA Cup, and they couldn't repeat the feat while he wore their distinctive tangerine shirts. They were runners up to

Manchester United in the First Division in the 1955/56 season and he was voted Young Player of the Year in 1959.

It was the supreme irony that one of the best players of the era went to school where football was discouraged – but Jimmy played rugby and cricket, and was an accomplished athlete. In football he was to make his under-23 level debut against the Scots at Hillsborough in February 1956, though by January 1956 Jimmy was otherwise occupied with National Service, with the King's Own Royal Regiment. It was then that Corporal Armfield was called up for the other type of National Service, with a shirt with three lions on the front and No. 2 on the back.

At senior level Jimmy won forty-three caps for England starting with a match against the Brazilians, and it was in the 1962 World Cup that he was given the accolade of the best right back in the world. Jimmy was in the squad for the 1966 World Cup finals but had been injured so didn't make an appearance.

Blackpool became his home and he married Anne Ashurst in the late spring of 1958; they had two sons, and now have grandchildren.

Jimmy was unsettled at Blackpool in 1963 and made a written transfer request; this was as a result of a long-running dispute over pay. But it was settled amicably by the directors and the foundation was laid by Jimmy himself, saying that there was no 'bad blood' between himself and the board. In the event he didn't leave Blackpool (much to Arsenal's disappointment) and he played his final game of 569 on 1 May 1971, in front of a crowd of over

30,000 against Manchester United at Bloomfield Road. He didn't score in this match but his goal tally was six for his career.

The management career he pursued after his playing days was slightly less difficult, he said, than lion-taming. Jimmy took the reins at Bolton Wanderers in 1971, steering them to promotion as Third Division champions. Then with the (some say premature and some say over-due) departure of Brian Clough from Leeds United, Jimmy was appointed manager with Don Howe as his second-in-command. Leeds got to the final of the European Cup in 1975 but were defeated by Bayern Munich.

However, he wasn't happy as a manager so decided to pursue a career in journalism. He served the *Daily Express* readers from 1979 until 1991 and joined the BBC shortly afterwards. On Radio Five, Jimmy presents football commentary and analysis.

To start his collection of awards he was awarded the OBE in 2000 for his services to football and the CBE in 2010 for his services to the folk of Blackpool: he has many local charitable interests, and plays the organ at his local church. When asked if he was a pillar of the local community he said he thought 'pillock' might be a more apt description. His autobiography, *Right Back at the Beginning*, was released in 2004 and, like Jimmy himself, didn't have a bad word to say about anyone.

His health has played up in recent years: he fought off a lymphoma in the throat with painful chemotherapy but, as already noted, he is one of life's winners. The Professional Footballers' Association (PFA) gave him an award for 'Merit' and the Football League recognised his 'Outstanding Contribution' to the game. Jimmy appears in the Football Hall of Fame.

He did finally get a winner's medal for his 1966 contribution in 2009 with the rest of the 1966 squad. Had he not turned professional footballer he was to read Economics at Liverpool University, but it was Lancaster University who honoured him with a degree in 2011, a little later than he intended. Again later than he intended he got his hands on the FA Cup, but only to present it to John Terry, Chelsea Captain, in 2012. He still regularly attends Bloomfield Road stadium and his name is etched in the seats in one of the stands.

15

Gerry Byrne – Defender: Left Back

Gerald Byrne was born in Liverpool on 29 August 1938 and, like Jimmy Armfield above, he was a one-club player with the not-so-mighty-when-he-joined-them Liverpool Football Club. He joined the club straight from school aged fifteen in 1953: Gerry impressed the then manager Don Welsh who, the day after his seventieth birthday, offered him a full professional contract. So on 30 August 1955 he was to look forward to a career in a red shirt and white shorts with a red stripe down the side – changed to an all-red strip later, as Bill Shankly thought it looked more frightening!

It was just over two years later that Gerry made the trek down to The Valley in South London for a ninety-minute nightmare on his debut: Liverpool were beaten by

Charlton Athletic by five goals to nil. In February 1962 he got on the score sheet for the first time in a win over Brighton at Anfield. Liverpool were in the Second Division in those days and had just passed the second anniversary of the arrival from Huddersfield Town of the man who would make them a great side, Bill Shankly. Bill had assessed the potential of the players in his new squad and sold most of them, but he kept Gerry – who had been on the transfer list – and a young inside forward called Roger Hunt. Gerry Byrne formed a solid defence with Ronnie Moran and, later, with Chris Lawler at his side, while Ron Yeats in front saved Tommy Lawrence from having to make many a save.

Liverpool were soon to be champions of the Second Division and so promoted to the First. Of the forty-two games in the 1962/63 season, Gerry played in thirty-eight. They finished eight points clear of Leyton Orient and had the best goal average in the Football League.

The following season Liverpool finished a comfortable eighth while the League Championship was celebrated 400 yards away at Goodison Park. By that time though Gerry had made the Liverpool No. 2 shirt his own, and the following year the championship title left Everton and came the 400 yards to Anfield.

But it was in the FA Cup campaign of 1964/65 that Gerry showed that he was a player of class, skill and courage equal to the ten players who surrounded him. It was in the FA Cup final of 1965: very early on he went for a fifty-fifty ball with Leeds United's captain Bobby Collins, only three minutes from kick-off. Gerry broke his shoulder but he played on, even through an extra time of thirty minutes. He also swore club trainer Bob Paisley to secrecy to keep the injury away from Bill Shankly's ears. Bill was later to say that it was his courage that won the cup. Liverpool won by two goals to one, and Gerry managed to conceal the injury from the Leeds players. Watching the game now his arm seems to hang limp. The pain would finish most of us off, but not Gerry Byrne.

If the 1953 final came to be known as the Stanley Matthews final (by all but Stanley) then the 1964/65 final should be called the Gerry Byrne final. But the list of players injured in finals, like him, with no choice but to play on, was growing and soon the FA was to allow substitutes in games.

At Anfield the following Tuesday night Gerry and the team paraded the FA Cup in front of the Kop and on front of the visiting Inter Milan contingent, who seemed more than a little nervous. Liverpool won this European Cup match – but they lost the second leg.

Gerry was back the following season, when Liverpool won the League Championship again. Roger Hunt and the late Geoff Strong were the force up front but at the back they had the best defensive record in the league, letting in a mere thirty-four goals. So it was no surprise when master striker Roger Hunt, master defender Gerry Byrne and master wingman (midfielder in disguise) Ian Callaghan were called up to join Alf Ramsey and the gang for the 1966 World Cup finals in London.

Gerry had played for the full England side on his debut against the Scots in 1963 and was in front of another debutant that day in Gordon Banks. But competition in '66 was fierce and if the team were winning, which they were, Alf Ramsey would be loath to make any changes, and didn't. So Gerry didn't get an appearance in London in 1966, but did pick up his winner's medal later, forty years after he hung up his boots.

He had three more seasons at Anfield before he had to retire. The injury to his collar bone caused him few further problems, but it was the injury he sustained at Leicester City in August 1966, to his knee, that proved the beginning of the end. He played 333 games for Liverpool and scored four goals.

'If you heard him speak three times in a season you were lucky ... [but] when on the pitch he was superb' (Ron Yeats).

'The likes of Peter Thompson, Ian St John, Kevin Keegan and Steve Heighway were the ones who caught the eye. But the best professional of the lot was Gerry Byrne' (Bill Shankly, 1975).

Gerry lives in quiet (how else?) retirement in Wales.

16

Martin Peters – Midfield: Attack

Martin Stanford Peters was born on 8 November 1943 in Plaistow: although well into Essex it is served by the Tube. He would score the goal in the 1966 final that oh-so-nearly brought victory within the ninety minutes. He also played in the 1970 World Cup finals in Mexico and pulled on club shirts for West Ham United, Tottenham Hotspur, Norwich City and Sheffield United. He was briefly manager at Sheffield United but after 1984 his long-term future was in insurance rather than football.

It is probably no surprise that he became the most expensive footballer in the country, when a part-exchange deal was struck with West Ham to take him to White Hart Lane and Jimmy Greaves went to West Ham. He had, quite simply, the lot. He could kick well and pass accurately with either foot, and could head the ball; he had great movement so he was difficult for markers to get to grips with. And he was known as a bit of a free-kick specialist.

At West Ham United he played in every position, and did replace the goalkeeper in one early game. Alf Ramsey reflected on his skill after a one-all draw with Scotland in the 1968 European Championships – Martin had ended a useful move which saw Mike Summerbee of Manchester City, on his debut, form the link between the left flank and Ray Wilson with Martin who scored: Alf suggested he was ten years ahead of his time.

Like Geoff Hurst, Martin was a product of Ted Fenton's foresight and he signed him as an apprentice for West Ham in 1959.

He made his debut late in the 1961/62 season, on Good Friday when they beat Cardiff City at home by four goals to one. Martin was to play only five games that season. Early in September of the following season Martin scored his first goal for the club in a six-one win at Maine Road, home to Manchester City.

He played in thirty-two league matches in 1963/64 but not in any cup matches in West Ham United's winning year. The following year he became a regular and West Ham won the European Cup Winners' Cup. He made a useful trio with Ronnie Boyce and Eddie Bovington.

West Ham narrowly missed out on a third trophy in as many seasons in the Football League Cup in the 1965/66 season – still a two-legged home and away final. They were beaten on aggregate by West Bromwich Albion despite Martin scoring: final score, five-three. That was the last season in which the Football League Cup final was played as home and away and it became a one-off final thereafter.

He got his own back, so to speak, a couple of years later when he scored his one and only hat-trick for West Ham against West Bromwich. In that 1968/69 season he scored a total of twenty-four goals in forty-eight games.

It has been claimed that he felt he was in the shadow of Bobby Moore and Geoff Hurst at West Ham, but this didn't prevent him becoming England's most expensive player. When he moved to pastures new, he was valued at a record-breaking £200,000 and Tottenham released Jimmy Greaves, valued at £50,000, with the rest in cash. He made his debut and scored his first goal for Tottenham in a one-all draw with Coventry City at White Hart Lane. In 1971 he won a Football League Cup winner's tankard (not medal) when they beat Aston Villa by two goals to nil.

The UEFA Cup had replaced the Inter-City Fairs Cup and Tottenham beat Wolverhampton Wanderers by the odd goal in five on aggregate in 1972. Then in 1973 he added another Football League Cup winner's tankard when they beat Norwich City by a goal to nil. His final stint in Europe came in another UEFA Cup final when Tottenham were defeated by Dutch club Feyenoord.

He then left Tottenham to join his former West Ham United teammate John Bond who was manager of Norwich City; this was March 1975 and the fee was £50,000.

Martin was now thirty-one but still had plenty in the tank, and newly promoted Norwich City were helped enormously to consolidate their position in the top flight with Martin on board. He made over 200 appearances and had a testimonial match against a team made up of the 1966 squad with a few others.

He had the accolade of being Norwich City's Player of the Year two years running and in 1978 he was awarded an MBE for his services to football. He is in Norwich City's Hall of Fame.

Then, in July 1980, off he went north to join Sheffield United, this time he was player/coach. It was thought that he would replace Harry Haslam as manager, since Mr Haslam wasn't enjoying good health.

Martin's first appearance for Sheffield United came in an Anglo-Scottish Cup match against Hull City, and his league debut was on the first day of the 1980/81 season in a Third Division match against Carlisle United: it was a three-nil win and he scored his first goal for the new club.

On 17 January 1981 Harry Haslam retired, so Martin took the manager's role. His final league game as a player came at Gillingham on that day. Sheffield United were twelfth in the Third Division and had twelve more games to play. But they didn't do at all well and won only three of their outstanding fixtures. They were relegated to the Fourth Division and Martin resigned.

His career had seen him compete in 882 games and score 220 goals. He was also lucky with few injuries.

Martin made his debut for England at Wembley on 4 May 1966, against Yugoslavia. Alf Ramsey had made no secret that he thought Martin world class and he laid on the pass that saw Jimmy Greaves score. He nearly scored himself on a couple of occasions. He played twice more before Alf named him in his twenty-two man squad for the World Cup finals of 1966. He had scored in the 'warm-up' game against Finland in Helsinki and was in the team for the next game against Norway.

Martin didn't play in the dour no-score draw against Uruguay in the opening game. For the next clash, Alan Ball and John Connelly were sidelined for Martin and Terry Paine: Terry was an out-and-out winger so one wonders at Alf's thinking. However, England won by two goals to nil. Martin stayed in the line-up against France and strangely Terry Paine was replaced by Ian Callaghan, who played more of a winger's role in those days. Again England won, but disaster had struck when Jimmy Greaves took a fair gash to his leg. From then on it was the West Ham three and eight others. But Alf had seemed to hit on a winning formula with Martin in the side.

In the quarter-final the inch-perfect cross to Geoff Hurst in space was the decisive strike against Argentina, and he was part of the masterpiece of a game against Portugal in the semi-finals. This match had an hour's play before even a foul was called.

Martin was in the final eleven for the showdown with West Germany whom they had beaten at Wembley a couple of months earlier, courtesy of Nobby Stiles.

The final could have gone either way. Luck eventually went more with England, though not many people would have said that with five seconds or so of the ninety minutes left. Not long before that Alan Ball took a corner which found its way to Geoff Hurst's feet just on the edge of the eighteen-yard box: he tried a rather optimistic shot and the ball bounced out of danger off Wolfgang Weber's foot. But it fell back into danger when it presented itself to Martin and he was close enough to goal to shoot with intent rather than simple optimism – fifteen minutes to go and England take the lead. There was then the equaliser for the West Germans and as England kicked off again the ball hadn't left the centre circle when full time was blown. Two goals in extra time meant Martin had done what only one other English footballer has done before by scoring a goal in a World Cup final.

So for the next few years Martin's name was synonymous with the England squad and by the time the 1970 World Cup finals in Mexico came about he had won thirty-eight caps. He played in all three group games, and his creativity came to the fore in the quarter-final tie with, again, West Germany. Early in the second half he ran through from behind a defender to kick England into a two-nil lead. However there was no error in Martin and Bobby Charlton being substituted – the West German fightback had begun and when it ended England were out of the tournament.

He reached the milestone of his fiftieth cap in 1972 in the European Championships when England beat Switzerland in Basle, but he missed the return match at Wembley the following month. He was on duty when West Germany triumphed at Wembley to effectively knock England out the following April.

Martin scored the only goal in a win over Scotland

on 19 May 1973, which took his international tally to twenty goals. England were not sharp in the qualifying stages for the 1974 World Cup finals and failed to qualify: in fact a dive in the game against Poland to win a penalty demonstrated how low the form and morale among the international set up had become.

His penultimate game for England was against Portugal in Lisbon which finished goalless, and was Alf Ramsey's last. On 18 May 1974 he won his sixty-seventh and final cap for England in a two-nil defeat by the Scots at Hampden Park.

When Martin finished his footballing career in 1984 he went into the insurance business, where he stayed, though he did join the board of directors at Tottenham Hotspur in 1998. He has also worked at both Upton Park and White Hart Lane in a hospitality role – his children and grandchildren are West Ham United supporters.

He met Kathleen Ward in a Dagenham bowling alley in 1961 and they married in 1964. Lee-Ann was born in 1965 and Grant in 1970. Martin and Kathleen live in Shenfield in Essex.

17

Ron Flowers – Midfield: Supporting Defence

Ronald Flowers was the oldest member of the 1966 squad and was born on 28 July 1934 in Doncaster in Yorkshire. He spent fifteen years with Wolverhampton Wanderers and latterly Northampton Town.

Like many of his contemporaries he was taken along to the railway works at the appropriate age to learn a trade. But his father was fanatical about football so he wasn't there for long! Ron had a brother, John, who also played professional football (Stoke City, Doncaster Rovers, and Port Vale) and Ron's uncle played for Doncaster Rovers and Tranmere Rovers.

Ron was taken up and prepared for greatness by probably the best servant Wolverhampton Wanderers ever had (as player and manager), Stan Cullis, and made his debut in September 1952 as Wolverhampton Wanderers took on Blackpool at Molineux. They were beaten by five goals to two – but Ron scored.

Stan Cullis steered his side to bring Ron personally three League Championships and an FA Cup win.

Ron was more of an attacking midfielder and scored thirty-seven times in 515 appearances. His strike rate for England was about one in five, with ten goals from his forty-nine appearances. His debut was against France but England lost by a goal to nil. Another stalwart from Molineaux, Billy Wright, made more consecutive appearances for England but Ron still knocked up forty between late 1958 and 1963. For the England under-23 level side he made four appearances and when he graduated to full international he was made captain for three matches.

He was in the World Cup squad for the Chilean finals in 1962. He equalised from the penalty spot when England were beaten by two goals to one by Hungary, and scored again from the penalty spot when England defeated Argentina. Ron played in all four of England's games and they were eventually knocked out by Brazil in the quarter-finals.

In October 1962 Hillsborough was the venue for European Nations Cup game, the first leg against France, and Ron scored the only English goal in a one-all draw – the first goal England had scored in the tournament.

He made his final appearance in an England shirt in Oslo in Norway on 29 June 1966. England won by six goals to one and this was two games before the opening of the 1966 World Cup finals. However when Jack Charlton looked doubtful the night before the final, Alf told Ron to be ready, but it was not to be.

In 1967 he joined Northampton Town just after the season had started and he was later to be made player/manager. He made sixty-two appearances for Northampton and scored four goals. He left for Wellington Town, as player/manager. Wellington was later called Telford United who also had two others from the squad – Geoff Hurst and Gordon Banks as their managers later, too.

But he wasn't too well suited to management and before long he wanted to get back to Wolverhampton. He opened Ron Flowers Sports which trades to this day in the town under the management of Ron's son.

Before all of this, though, he did his National Service in the RAF and married Yvonne Hart in the early spring of 1957.

He also holds a record for England, which he now shares with Alan Shearer, as the best penalty taker for the national side, converting all six he took.

18

Norman Hunter – Defence: Half Back

Norman Hunter was born in Gateshead, County Durham in October 1943 and was an absolute rock in the mighty Leeds United defence from 1962 until 1976. In total he made 540 appearances for Don Revie's men and scored eighteen goals. He originally joined Leeds United when he was fifteen and gave up the opportunity of a job in electrics. Norman made his first-team debut for Leeds in 1962 when they were in the Second Division and formed a partnership at the back with Jack Charlton which lasted for a decade. By 1964 they had won the Second Division championship so were promoted to the First Division and had a good first season in the top, only losing the League Championship to Manchester United on goal average (goal difference – goals scored *minus* goals conceded – came along later, goal average was goals scored *divided* by goals conceded). In the same season Leeds had a marathon FA Cup run but were pipped to the cup in extra time at Wembley by Liverpool: Roger Hunt scored for Liverpool before Billy Bremner equalised for Leeds; Ian St John got the winner seven minutes before the end of extra time.

Norman made his England debut in a match against Spain in Madrid three weeks before Christmas 1965, coming on as a substitute for Joe Baker. This game is worth some consideration even if it is slightly off-topic: Alf Ramsey had attempted to build a team with two midfielders reaching out to the flanks; they were supported by the full backs overlapping, a role that George Cohen and Ray Wilson relished. And it worked – the back four of George, Ray, Jack Charlton and Bobby Moore were well settled so Alf could now look at attack. And the 'wingless wonders', as they became known, worked because until that game against Scotland in 1967 England had a run of seventeen games without defeat. One problem Norman had was that his usual position to the left and slightly forward of the left back was the same position as Bobby Moore occupied. Subsequently Norman didn't get his next cap until the one-nil defeat of Austria in Vienna in May 1967. However from about May 1968 he began to collect his caps much more frequently.

He had already picked up winner's medals at club level. Leeds United won the Football League Cup in 1968, the Inter-City Fairs Cup in 1968 and again in 1971. The prize of football, the League Championship, went to Elland Road in 1969. There were a few disappointments along the way for Leeds but they won the FA Cup in 1972 and Norman attended the Royal Box twice as he helped Mick Jones climb the steps. It was this game when 'Bites yer Legs' became his nickname – his tackle was always robust.

More disappointments came in the FA Cup final to Sunderland and then in the Cup Winners' Cup, but there was some suggestion of impropriety among officials, with fixes in European games.

A new award came Norman's way in 1974 when he was elected as the first PFA Players' Player of the Year.

Gordon McQueen was brought in to replace Jack Charlton, who had gone into management, which gave Norman a new lease of life. Leeds started the season 1973/74 with a twenty-nine-match unbeaten run that led them to the title. He was a member of the Leeds side that reached the 1975 European Cup final, which Leeds lost two to nil against Bayern Munich; Jimmy Armfield was Leeds United manager at this time.

After 540 Football League appearances for Leeds he still had a bit of petrol in the tank so signed for Bristol City in 1976 for £40,000. He remained there for three years, making 108 appearances and scoring four goals. His final game for Bristol City was against Leeds United.

In 1979 he signed for Barnsley for whom he played thirty-one matches before he finally hung up his boots in 1983. By then he had spent a couple of seasons as manager of the club.

Norman scored the winning goal against Spain in England's quarter-final in the 1968 European Championships. He then started in both the one-nil semi-final defeat to Yugoslavia and the two-nil victory over the Soviet Union in the third place play-off. He was in Alf Ramsey's squad for the 1970 World Cup in Mexico, but only came on late as a substitute for Martin Peters in the three-two defeat by West Germany.

In 1973, he was in the England team which needed to win their last qualifying tie for the 1974 World Cup in West Germany. The opposition at Wembley was Poland, who just needed a draw to qualify. It was still goalless when he made a tackle on the royal box side of the half-way line, he didn't come out of the tackle too well, and Poland went on the attack, scoring completely against the run of play. Allan Clarke equalised with a penalty but England could not score again, and the one-all draw saw them miss out on a place at the World Cup. He had a lot of support later from the man he replaced for England, Bobby Moore.

Norman was appointed manager of Barnsley in September 1980 and took them to second place in the Third Division in the 1980/81 season, so they were promoted. They managed sixth in the Second Division the following season and would possibly have done better with later season consistency. The following season they made a promising start but struggled. In February 1984, Norman and Barnsley parted company: but within a week he was appointed first team coach at West Bromwich Albion, a position he held until June 1985.

He later moved back to Yorkshire to manage Rotherham United but this didn't work out at all well and he left in December 1987. Finally he took over at Leeds United but only as caretaker manager following the departure of Billy Bremner and in a very short time Howard Wilkinson was appointed as full-time manager. In 1989 he became a coach at Bradford City but was sacked in February 1990.

More recently Norman has been engaged on the after-dinner circuit recounting what life was like in the real world. He worked for BBC Radio Leeds and Yorkshire Radio commenting on Leeds games. In 1998 the Football League included him on its list of 100 League Legends.

He married Susanne Harper in June 1968 and they had a son and a daughter; they now have grandchildren. He has also taken time out to teach children the basics of football in Leeds schools.

Although it is difficult to confirm where the following piece of banter came from, it nicely sums up Norman's 'Bites yer Legs' reputation: when he was laid up injured and someone told the Leeds United trainer Les Cocker that Norman had broken a leg, his only question was: 'Whose leg?'

19

Terry Paine – Striker: Winger

Terence Lionel Paine was born on 23 March 1939 in Winchester, Hampshire and is best known for his career with Southampton, for whom he played for eighteen seasons making a club record of over 800 appearances. He later played for Hereford United, and briefly at Cheltenham Town as a player-manager. Terry was primarily a winger, but also took a midfield or striker's role.

He started out as a youth player with local club Winchester City, before signing professionally with Southampton in 1956, and quite quickly became a regular for the team. In 1960 Southampton were Third Division champions and six years later they won promotion to the First Division. He left the club in 1974 to play for Hereford United, who won promotion into the Third Division in

1976, and hung up his boots at the end of the 1976/77 season. He later took the job as manager – though he played a couple of times – at Cheltenham Town and in the 1980s had a few coaching jobs as well as becoming a pundit for South African TV.

When he left school he worked for British Railways in their Eastleigh depot and played amateur football for Winchester City. He had trials for Portsmouth and Arsenal but Winchester's manager was Harry Osman who had played for Southampton and alerted manager Ted Bates to Terry's potential. In August 1956 he signed amateur forms and then professional forms in February the following year. He made his reserve team debut against Bristol Rovers and in March 1957 – actually on his eighteenth birthday – he made his league debut in a one-all draw with Aldershot.

He had pace and ability and either foot was useful, and he had the confidence of a seasoned campaigner. This didn't go down too well with some of the senior members of Southampton's squad but they were impressed, nonetheless. He could dribble and could cross with pin-point accuracy.

In March 1960 he entered the international scene playing at under-23 level against Holland at Hillsborough. He scored in the five goals to two victory, this was the first of four under-23 level caps he won.

He did have a stint in goal when the Southampton goalkeeper, Ron Reynolds, broke an ankle in a league match on the opening day of the 1961/62 season. He was beaten twice before handing the gloves to a teammate – I couldn't find any further records of his goalkeeping.

With his opposite winger, John Sydenham, they fed two of the better old-school centre forwards, Ron Davies and Martin Chivers. And he adapted well to midfield after the phasing out of wingers, feeding youngster Mike Channon.

Terry also had an uncanny way of avoiding injuries and his career shows an almost complete continuity, completing seven seasons without a break. He made 709 league appearances and 102 cup and others. He scored 187 goals at club level.

He was made team captain and received his first full England cap in a four-two victory against Czechoslovakia in Bratislava on 29 May 1963 – Alf Ramsey's fourth game. Terry scored a hat-trick in an eight goals to three defeat of Northern Ireland. His final cap came in the 1966 finals in the group match against Mexico.

He received the MBE in 1977 and his total of 819 matches was then a record for an outfield player. He took his expertise into management with Cheltenham Town.

Southampton's new stadium St Mary's has named a hospitality suite after him and he had several business interests in the town. He also served as a councillor. He was to meet another politician in Prime Minister Gordon Brown when he was presented with his World Cup winner's medal in 2009.

He still works as a pundit in South Africa specialising in the English games, mainly in the Premiership and European Competitions. He is also Honorary President of Southampton Football Club.

Terry got married a couple of times . . .

20

Ian Callaghan – Striker: Winger

Ian Robert Callaghan was born 10 April 1942 in Toxteth, Liverpool and holds the record for most appearances for Liverpool, the club he supported as a youngster, joined as an apprentice at the end of March 1960, and for whom he made his debut just under three weeks later! That was against Bristol Rovers at Anfield, and the score was four-nil.

A right winger, Ian was a regular in the team from 1961 onwards. The club was promoted from the Second Division as champions in 1961/62 under Bill Shankly. Ian appeared twenty-three times that season and also scored his first goal for the club against Preston North End at Deepdale on 4 November 1961.

He became a major part of the side which finished eighth in their first season back in Division One. The following year,

1963/64, Liverpool won the League Championship by four points over north-west rivals Manchester United and five over Merseyside rivals and reigning league champions Everton.

In the 1964/65 season, they could only finish seventh in the defence of their title but did reach the FA Cup final against league runners-up Leeds United. With the match goalless at full time, extra time followed. Roger Hunt scored for Liverpool three minutes into extra time but Billy Bremner equalised for Leeds two minutes later. The game seemed to be heading for a replay until Ian broke down the right, and fearing he had gone too far, brought the ball back from the by-line. It was met by a diving Ian St John who headed home from close range.

The 1965/66 season saw another League Championship but this was tempered by defeat in the European Cup Winners' Cup final as Borussia Dortmund won by the odd goal in three at Hampden Park.

In the 1966 finals of the World Cup, Ian played in the group game against France which England won two-nil, but was left out of the side as it progressed, with Alf preferring a system which didn't favour wingers.

In the late 1960s, as Bill Shankly set about reorganising the Liverpool set-up, Ian moved to a more central midfield role.

Liverpool reached the 1971 FA Cup final, losing two-one to Arsenal after extra time. The 1972/73 campaign saw Liverpool achieve a League and UEFA Cup double, winning the league by three points over Arsenal and defeating German team Borussia Mönchengladbach in the UEFA Cup final, taking a three-nil first-leg lead.

In 1974 Liverpool won the FA Cup again, beating Newcastle United. Ian was named the Football Writers' Footballer of the Year and was awarded the MBE for his services to football.

In 1976 at the age of thirty-four he played in Bob Paisley's side which won another League and UEFA Cup double. He played in all the European matches and missed just two league games. Queens Park Rangers were top with Liverpool having one game left to play, away at Wolverhampton Wanderers. Liverpool trailed by a goal to nil with just fourteen minutes remaining before Kevin Keegan equalised, John Toshack put them into the lead and Ray Kennedy added a third goal. The UEFA Cup final saw the Anfield club face Bruges of Belgium. Liverpool took a slender three-two lead to Belgium and held Bruges to a goal a piece draw, to take the trophy for second time.

In the 1976/77 season, at thirty-five, he won his third and fourth England caps. His first two were in the run-up to and against France in the 1966 World Cup. The gap of 11 years 49 days, and 108 internationals are records. Ian was the last member of the 1966 World Cup winning squad to appear for England.

Liverpool won the League again in 1977, beating Manchester City into second spot by a single point. Manchester United stood in their way for a double and beat Liverpool by two goals to one in the FA Cup final. Ian came on in the second half and impressed Bob Paisley enough for him to keep him in the side for the European Cup final win in Rome.

Ian played one more season for Liverpool, appearing in forty-one league and cup matches. At the end of the 1977/78 season, Liverpool retained the European Cup, he was a non-playing substitute.

In the autumn of 1978, after 856 first team appearances, he left the club for Swansea City, helping them to two consecutive promotions. He also played in the United States for Fort Lauderdale Strikers alongside Gordon Banks and George Best. He played for Canberra City, Cork United and although he signed for Sandefjord of Norway he didn't play for them as he couldn't get a work permit. His final port of call was Crewe Alexandra where he set an all time record of eighty-eight FA Cup appearances. He retired at the age of thirty-nine in 1982 though it was injury and not age that finally ended his career.

Ian married Linda Foulder in the late spring of 1969 and they had two daughters, Samantha in 1970 and Suzanne in 1974. Linda and Ian were always close even though they divorced, and he was devastated when Linda passed away in 2009.

He started an insurance sales business and can still be seen at Anfield as he is a regular visitor to the club he still supports. He is the president of the Official Liverpool FC Fan club. Venerated by the Anfield faithful, he was voted in at fifteen in the '100 Players Who Shook The Kop' poll in 2006.

21

Roger Hunt – Striker

Roger Hunt was born on 20 July 1938 in Golborne, Lancashire. Just over a week after his twentieth birthday he was signed by Phil Taylor for Liverpool. It was Scunthorpe United who were first on the receiving end of his strikes when he scored in the sixty-forth minute of a Second Division match on 9 September 1959. This gave Liverpool a two to nil victory and Roger was to score a further 285 goals for the club in the league and cup competitions, which was a club record.

When Bill Shankly was appointed manager of Liverpool in December of 1959 he set about reforming his squad and let a total of twenty-four players go, but Roger was one of the few he retained to build the club up towards First Division strength. They gained their promotion to the First Division in 1962; they had just missed out over the past few seasons.

In the 1961/62 season Roger really began to turn up the screw and scored an average of a goal a game for the forty-one appearances he made that season. His tally included five hat-tricks as Liverpool romped to an eight-point lead to win the Second Division championship. And the First Division was where Roger established himself as a true goal-scoring icon. He was the club's highest scorer as they won the League Championship in 1965/66. In the FA Cup the story wasn't very different. In Liverpool's cup-winning season of 1964/65 he scored four goals in the FA Cup campaign. Then in the final, or at any rate, in extra time, he scored the goal that broke the deadlock: Ian St John got the winner against Leeds United. In Europe the following season Liverpool made it through to the final and Roger scored Liverpool's goal in the two-one defeat, to Borrussia Dortmund.

On 22 August 1964, on the first edition of *Match of the Day*, Liverpool ('in the dark shirts') took on Arsenal at Anfield. Early in the first half Peter Thompson put a little too much power on his cross but it found Ian Callaghan who chested the ball down before a very delicate chip for Roger to hook an up and under into the far corner. So Roger scored in the three-two home win, this was the first goal seen on *Match of the Day*.

He became Liverpool's record goal scorer on 7 November 1967 in an Inter-City Fairs Cup match with TSV 1860 Munchen of West Germany, in which he scored his 242nd goal for the club. His final tally for Liverpool was 286 goals by the time he left the club to join Bolton Wanderers in 1969. The record was broken twenty-three years later by Ian Rush.

Roger was capped thirty-four times for England; making his debut under Walter Winterbottom in April 1962 whilst a Second Division player. This was in a friendly against Austria at Wembley, and he scored as England won three to one. He then went to the 1962 World Cup finals in Chile, but didn't play.

In the 1966 World Cup finals, Roger and club mates Ian Callaghan and Gerry Byrne were selected for the twenty-two man squad, Roger being one of three forwards selected for the tournament. He initially partnered Tottenham Hotspur striker Jimmy Greaves up front but, following Jimmy's leg injury, he played alongside Geoff Hurst. He played in all six games, scoring three times, as England went on to win the Jules Rimet trophy at Wembley.

Roger is the player who Geoff Hurst always mentions when discussing his controversial second goal in the final, when the ball hit the crossbar and bounced down. Geoff always said that Roger, who was the closest player to the ball, would have followed up to score himself if he had been in any doubt, but he turned away in celebration of a certain goal.

After retiring from football in 1972, Roger joined his family's haulage company and in 1975 became a sitting member of the pools panel, who predict results of games postponed because of adverse weather in order for pools players to still win.

In 2000, he joined fellow 1966 heroes Alan Ball, George Cohen, Nobby Stiles and Ray Wilson in receiving the MBE, the 'forgotten five.'

Roger was inducted into the English Football Hall of Fame in 2006, recognising his achievements in the English game. He was voted at thirteen by Liverpool fans in the '100 Players Who Shook The Kop' poll in the same year.

With Bolton Wanderers he scored twenty-four goals in seventy-six games from 1969 to 1972.

He married Patricia O'Brien in 1959 but they parted and divorced in 1981. They had two children: David was born in 1960 and Julie in 1965.

22

George Eastham – Midfield: Attack

George Edward Eastham was born on 23 September 1936 and played for Newcastle United, Arsenal and Stoke City. He was capped nineteen times at full international level. His father and uncle were professionals before him and George is one of only a handful of players whose father also played at international level. As a member of the 1966 squad he didn't play in any of the games.

His first professional kick was for a Northern Irish club, Ards, for whom his father was player/manager. Small and wiry, George played at inside forward and later in midfield.

He joined Newcastle United in autumn of 1956 and made his debut against Luton Town in a two-all draw in October of that year. He was to stay at St James' Park for four seasons, playing 125 games and scoring thirty-four goals. He won caps for the Football League and at under-23 level.

Off the pitch George wasn't happy. The accommodation the club provided wasn't good, he didn't like a secondary job the club had arranged and felt there were tensions with him playing at under-23 level. So when his contract expired he wouldn't sign a new one and asked for a transfer, but the club refused. They could retain his registration and just stop paying him. George said:

'Our contract could bind us to a club for life. Most people called it the "slavery contract". We had virtually no rights at all. It was often the case that the guy on the terrace not only earned more than us – though there's nothing wrong with that – he had more freedom of movement than us. People in business or teaching were able to hand in their notice and move on. We weren't. That was wrong.'

He withdrew his services at the end of the 1959/60 season, moving south to work in Guildford, Surrey. In October 1960 Newcastle United sold him to Arsenal for £47,500. But George thought the point was worth fighting and, backed by the PFA, he took the club to the High Court in 1963. He argued 'restraint of trade' with a claim for unpaid wages and bonuses. Mr Justice Wilberforce declined to rule on the claim for wages and bonuses, which was for Newcastle United's discretion. But he ruled that the so-called 'retain-and-transfer' system was unreasonable, which effectively changed the British transfer market. Players were given fairer terms and a tribunal was set up for disputes. George will forever be remembered for this conflict, which led to him being given the title of 'The Father of Modern Transfers'.

He made his eventual and belated debut for Arsenal against Bolton Wanderers on 10 December 1960, scoring twice in a five-one win. He became a regular for the side over the six seasons he was there, making 223 appearances and scoring forty-one goals. Over time, he changed from a forward to a midfield support role behind the main strike force.

George's international career progressed whilst at Highbury. He went to Chile with the 1962 World Cup squad, though he didn't play in the tournament. He nearly didn't get there – the Tannoy at Heathrow had to call repeatedly for him as the flight was closing. He had made his debut for England against Brazil on 8 May 1963 and made his final appearance against Denmark in a warm-up game the 1966 World Cup finals.

At Arsenal he was club captain but in 1966 Billy Wright departed and George, aged nearly thirty, looked for pastures new. Before the start of the 1966/67 season he joined Stoke City for £35,000. Under Tony Waddington Stoke combined young local talent with experience, and George was to spend eight seasons at Stoke. He also consolidated his coaching skills while on loan to South African side, Hellenic.

Back in England he was going strong at Stoke, who beat Chelsea to win the Football League Cup in 1971/72, with George scoring the winning goal. At thirty-five years 161 days, he was the oldest player to receive a winner's medal, or tankard.

He made 194 league appearances for Stoke, ten as a substitute, scoring four goals. George was to retire from playing in 1974, he was awarded the OBE for services to football just the year before.

His South African connection continued, as did his Stoke City role, and he returned to become Tony Waddington's assistant. When Tony resigned in March 1977 George was appointed manager but couldn't prevent relegation in at the end of the 1976/77 season. After failing to gain promotion back the following season he was sacked in January 1978.

In 1978, he quit professional football and emigrated to South Africa to set up his own sportswear business.

George married Pamela Lewis in the late spring of 1958 and they had three children, Christine, Susan and George. He is now chairman of the South African Arsenal Supporters' Club.

PUBLICITY AND PROMOTION

The Front Room Boys

The main link to the World Cup finals for us mere mortals at home was the television and the BBC, as the backbone of English broadcasting, had their most eloquent commentator on show, Kenneth Wolstenholme. The main attraction of Kenneth was his economy of words. He clearly he wanted the football to do the talking: he was merely the translator. Sadly that didn't last and the more ebullient commentators came along, annoying Brian Clough and no doubt countless others too. It was never to go back and now we have an entire panel of folk telling us what we've just seen.

Ironically in those primitive days of three channels it still seemed as though there was enough football to go round. We talked of little else and certainly in the summer of

1966 the World Cup was on the tip of everyone's tongue. Once the players were on the pitch, providing there wasn't too much physical stuff, we saw little of the trainers or managers. It was just us, the players and the telly – so the telly men became life-long fixtures in the subconscious. Hugh Johns was another who kept us on the edge of our seats: Hugh for independent television and Ken for the Beeb. Their mutual respect was to become apparent as the years went on, and the nostalgia merchants certainly helped.

Kenneth Wolstenholme was born in Bolton in Lancashire in July 1920 and went to Farnworth Grammar School, as did Alan Ball many years later.

Like Hugh Johns, Ken thought nothing of joining up when the war came along. He was in the RAF and ended up as an acting Squadron Leader. But he was never one to speak of his courage as an RAF pilot who flew 100 missions during the Second World War, for which he received the Distinguished Flying Cross and Bar. He flew his last mission in 1944 at just twenty-three.

On the 1966 lot he said: 'It wasn't just a team ... Alf Ramsey formed a football club in 1966. I felt privileged to be part of it.'

Martin Peters remarked: ' I worked a lot with Kenneth. He was part and parcel of the '66 team.'

Ken left the BBC in the early 1970s and it was with some disappointment that we tuned into a new theme tune and no Ken; there was nothing wrong with Barry Davies and John Motson but Ken was almost an establishment.

Lucky old Tyne Tees television got him for a while, but the sheepskin-coated holder of what looked like a milk stout (but was actually a microphone) faded from the telly but not the memories of '66.

His wife Joan Brownhill, whom he married in 1944, died in 1997. His last television appearance was on the quiz show *Weakest Link* and he was the first 'voted off'. He said he was shocked at being sent off that early.

Kenneth died in March 2002 and was survived by Lena of their two daughters, and grandchildren.

Hugh Johns was born in the rural town of Wantage in Berkshire in September 1922, so was just a few days short of his seventeenth birthday when war broke out. He served with the Fleet Air Arm and on demobilisation decided on an acting career. This didn't lead him to any great heights, and so he settled down eventually as a journalist, got married in 1950, and as a sports reporter for *The People* life seemed alright. But if his acting talent didn't lead him to greatness then the voice he cultivated had the right effect on the ear. Lew (later Sir, later Lord, and according to one former Luton Town director, one Eric Morecambe: 'Your royal highness …') Grade was a powerful television mogul and he decided Hugh would be a positive contribution to the Independent Stations. Hugh joined Associated Television which covered the Midlands area, so some attractive clubs were featured on what became a Sunday afternoon staple, *Star Soccer*.

But Hugh was to join up with his colleagues from the other independent stations and, since Brian Moore took the lead role and was based in a studio, Hugh donned his headphones and his microphone and became our link to the Wembley terraces for the 1966 World Cup finals. He had some pleasant company in the commentary box, such as Tommy Docherty and Billy Wright.

Hugh completed four World Cup final tournaments and once admitted that the skills of the Dutch superstar Johan Cruyff had him spellbound. He will always be remembered as the 'voice of Midlands football' and in 2002 Brian Clough presented him with a golden microphone.

After just over fifty years of marriage Joan died in November 2003 and Hugh followed her four years later. He said he had 'smoked twenty or thirty fags a day for most of my life and was one of Mr Booth's [gin] best customers'. As a resident of South Wales he could indulge himself with Brains beers.

As Geoff Hurst somehow managed to trot round to Alan Ball after his third goal had nearly broken the net, Hugh was there to tell us Geoff had scored a hat-trick – the one and only time that *had* happened; the one and only time that *has* happened.

He said later: 'It was a fabulous day though ... and I don't think many people would have realised the effort and emotions of that game and trying to relay that ... I remember being totally washed out at the end of it ... I went back to the Hendon Hall and had three large gins and went to bed. I was absolutely exhausted.'

Hugh and Joan had a son, Mark.

One newcomer in 1966 who, in various guises, has appeared in every World Cup finals tournament since, is the tournament mascot. For England it was the rather friendly and gentle-looking lion that walked on his hind-legs – World Cup Willie. He was to be the first official World Cup mascot and every finals tournament since has had one. Strangely, he sometimes wore the red white and blue of the Union Jack rather the red and white of St George.

Skiffle King (one would call him a musician in polite company) Lonnie Donegan even sang a song about him. He was the creation of artist Reg Hoye, who also worked on some of Enid Blyton's books, but he actually based Willie on his son, Leo. He went on to design other mascots, most notably a Red Devil for Manchester United. But it was all new back then, as Willie turned up on scarves, mugs and all of the paraphernalia we commonly see today, and World Cup Willie memorabilia fetches good prices today too. In one German magazine Willie is actually depicted drawing Mr Hoye.

Reg Hoye passed away in 1987.

Full Time – Match Reports

England qualified for the final tournament as hosts.

West Germany didn't have a tough time qualifying for the 1966 finals and shared a group with Sweden, who had been runners-up in 1958 but hadn't qualified in 1962, and Cyprus who had yet to qualify for the finals tournament. In November of 1964 West Germany drew one goal each with Sweden in Berlin. This was followed the next April with West Germany beating Cyprus by five goals to nil in Karlsruhe (home town of Oliver Bierhoff and Oliver Kahn who were yet to be born). On 5 May 1965 Sweden beat Cyprus three-nil; four months later the West German contingent went to Stockholm and won two-one. It started to look academic but Sweden won five-nil in Famagusta in Cyprus and a week later West Germany won six-nil;

it didn't help to change the venue to Nicosia. So the West Germans won three and drew one, and with seven points, qualified for the finals.

Come the finals they were in group two playing their ties either at Villa Park or Hillsborough. The other members of the group were Switzerland, Spain and Argentina. On 12 July West Germany ripped through the Swiss by five goals to nil and the following day Argentina just about crept through against Spain by two goals to one. Spain beat Switzerland by the odd goal in three and Argentina had a no-score draw with West Germany where Rafael Albrecht of Argentina was sent off. Argentina beat Switzerland two-nil before West Germany triumphed over Spain. So West Germany topped the group on goal average over the Argentinians: both had two wins and a draw.

England's group matches were all played at Wembley. There was a rather dull no-score draw with Uruguay, but then a reassuring two-nil win against Mexico. The two to nil win over France took Alf's men to the top of the group with five points. Uruguay also went through.

In the quarter-finals the West Germans thumped Uruguay four-nil at Hillsborough, but the Urugyans had two of their players sent off. England just about scraped home against a ten-man Argentina.

West Germany beat Lev Yashin's Russia by two goals to nil at Goodison Park but Igor Chislenko was dismissed. In the third place play-off Portugal beat Russia by two goals to one.

In the other semi-final the Portuguese star Eusébio scored from a penalty against England but was almost inconsolable as his team were knocked out. Eusébio da Silva Ferreira died of heart failure as this book was in preparation and was hailed as one of the greatest footballers of all time. During his professional career, he scored 733 goals in 745 matches. He won the Golden Boot with nine goals in the 1966 tournament.

So all eyes were on the host nation as the 1966 World Cup final kicked off. There were some magical moments in the first half and by half time the score was a goal each. At full time the score was two goals each. Jack Charlton had a foul awarded against him shortly before the end of ninety minutes – a harsh decision, but that's what the referee is there for. In extra time Hans Tilkowski couldn't stop Geoff Hurst's strike which hit the bar and bounced over the line before it came out – at least that's what the referee adjudged in consultation with his lineman. It was a goal – a tough call but he didn't shy away from it. West Germany were elegant in their play and graceful in defeat.

Will it Happen Again?

It sounds like the work of a party pooper to say that a repeat of 1966 could not happen today. But can we reproduce such a talented team? England is far more prosperous than it was in the Forties and Fifties, so sport might seem less attractive to the young. More and more English parents take their kids to school by car, whereas George Best was said to dribble a tennis ball to school and back. And parents don't want their kids out after dark. Cars dominate the streets and not kids kicking a football around. These trends must lessen the likelihood of young talent developing. Poorer countries can't offer their kids electronic gadgets and games but they can offer them sport, and at the moment the countries with less wealth do produce the better players, but not all of them. England's icons of the past ten or twenty years have still been capable of magic or wizardry, but the football calendar gets more and more congested, taking a toll on energy and injuries when the World Cup comes around.

But the mistakes of one generation don't necessarily influence another, and it is to be hoped that eventually people will tire of electronic games and fast lives and want to occupy open spaces again and compete in sports. Even today, if world-beating players can come from the English shores – Beckham, Rooney, Gerrard, Terry, Lampard, Walcott, Wilshere – to name but a few – then it must only be a matter of time before a team like the one discussed here becomes a possibility. And one thing that can be said for sure is that if the managers were left alone to manage, given the time to build and nurture a winning team, then another World Cup win becomes very much more likely. Sir Alf Ramsey's old boss at Ipswich Town, John Cobbold, believed a manager needed at least two years to settle in to produce the results. After only a few defeats many managers these days find themselves out of a job.

Far too many players at the top in England are not eligible to play for England, and chequebook team-building has certainly hampered the idea that today's school team captain will make it to the greatest clubs. It has been suggested that with so many Latin American and European players in the country this is a disadvantage. But why not turn this into an advantage, now that it is possible to see the strengths and weaknesses of such players and so many of them are playing within three or four hours of

Lancaster Gate. More importantly their skills are seen by English kids on the telly and it inspires them.

But all too often politics gets in the way of success: Sir Alf insisted on doing it his way, and winning it inadvertently lifted two fingers at some folk in the FA. Under Brian Clough another win might have been possible, but the day before he was interviewed for the vacant England Manager's job, the appointment of another candidate was apparently made. Brian could stand as an example of a potentially winning manager avoided because he didn't seem to be prepared to toe the 'party line'.

Nevertheless the history of football in this country, like history everywhere, tells us never to write off the unlikely. All we need are twenty-two players to form a squad and a management structure to bring out their best. Is this really too tall an order?

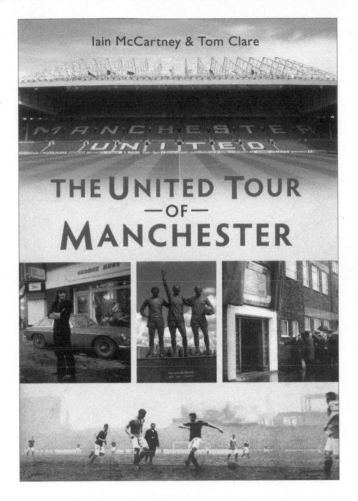

Iain McCartney & Tom Clare

THE UNITED TOUR
—OF—
MANCHESTER

THE UNITED TOUR OF MANCHESTER

Iain McCartney & Tom Clare

Ever wondered what the connection between Manchester United
and Bramhall Hall is? Do you know the exact location where the
Professional Footballers Association was founded? Where does the
first captain of Manchester United to lift a major trophy lie at rest?
The answers are to be found in this book, which takes you on the
United Tour of Manchester.

978 1 4456 1913 2
128 pages, full colour

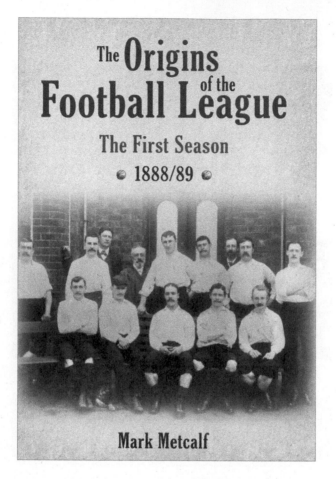

The Origins of the Football League
Mark Metcalf

'A valuable and timely record of the birth of one of football's most important institutions.' WHEN SATURDAY COMES

For the first time, the history of the Football League's first season is told in great depth, with reports on every match and profiles of all those who played.

978 1 4456 1881 4
224 pages, including 32 images

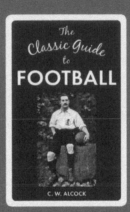